PRAISE FOR AUR

"Amy Leigh Mercree is a gifted healer and spiritual teacher. As my go-to medical intuitive, she opens the doors to expansive possibilities and optimal alignment for full body, mind, emotional, and spiritual health. This book is her masterpiece, and one the world has been waiting for."

— **Shannon Kaiser**, best-selling author of *The Self-Love Experiment*

"Step into a world of wonders with *Aura Alchemy*, where Amy Leigh Mercree's expertise as a medical intuitive fuses particle physics and spirituality in genius ways. Explore the magical connection between auras and elementary particles!"

— **Rebecca Campbell**, best-selling author of *Letters to a Starseed* and *Light Is the New Black*

"Forget emotional intelligence, this book is the future of energetic awareness! *Aura Alchemy* is a practical guide to energetic observations, awareness, and understanding. Spirituality collides with science to offer you real tools for the real day to help understand, clean, shift, raise, and protect your energy."

— **Emma Mildon**, best-selling author of *The Soul Searcher's Handbook* and *Evolution of Goddess*

"Amy Leigh Mercree's *Aura Alchemy* is the perfect book to understand energy from the angle of physics, metaphysics, fields, and color to help the reader live their best life, starting with their subtle body!"

— **Deanna Minich, Ph.D.**, author of *Whole Detox* and *The Complete Handbook of Quantum Healing*

"Prepare for a revelation with *Aura Alchemy*! Amy Leigh Mercree's expertise as a medical intuitive unveils the magical connection between auras and elementary particles, offering transformative manifestation insights."

— **George Lizos**, #1 best-selling author of *Lightworkers Gotta Work* and *Protect Your Light*

"In *Aura Alchemy*, Amy Leigh Mercree weaves words together like a mystic bursting with wisdom. In this book, you are taken on an enchanting journey and you experience Amy's magic as the powerful medical intuitive that she is."

— **Hannah Wallace**, host of the Finding Grace podcast, speaker, writer, and disability advocate

"*Aura Alchemy* is the ultimate resource for seeing, understanding, protecting, and working with the aura to improve every area of life. Amy masterfully combines her insight as a medical intuitive with quantum physics in a way anyone can understand; and through new insights and powerful exercises, she reveals an exciting way to manifest positive change."

— **Tammy Mastroberte**, author of *The Universe Is Talking to You*

"*Aura Alchemy* is a cosmic treasure that reveals the interplay between auras and particle physics. Amy Leigh Mercree's genius as a medical intuitive opens doors to new dimensions of manifestation."

— **Nicole Jardim**, certified women's health coach and author of *Fix Your Period*

"Amy is one of the best medical intuitives I know! I refer all my students to her! She's also a skilled, empowering, and supportive teacher and guide. You're in for a treat! You'll learn more about yourself, heal yourself and manifest with ease through *Aura Alchemy*!"

— **Dr. Deganit Nuur**, spiritual teacher, thought leader

AURA
ALCHEMY

ALSO BY AMY LEIGH MERCREE

*The Chakras and Crystals Cookbook: Juices,
Smoothies, Sorbets, Salads, and Crystal Infusions
to Empower Your Energy Centers*

*A Little Bit of Meditation:
An Introduction to Mindfulness*

*Recipes for Natural Living:
Essential Oils Handbook*

*Recipes for Natural Living:
Apple Cider Vinegar Handbook*

*A Little Bit of Mindfulness:
An Introduction to Being Present*

*The Mood Book: Crystals, Oils,
and Rituals to Elevate Your Spirit*

*A Little Bit of Goddess:
An Introduction to the Divine Feminine*

*A Little Bit of Chakras:
Your Personal Path to Energy Healing*

*A Little Bit of Meditation:
Your Personal Path to Mindfulness*

*A Little Bit of Mindfulness:
Your Personal Path to Awareness*

*100 Days to Calm: A Journal
for Finding Everyday Tranquility*

*The Healing Home: A Room-by-Room
Guide to Positive Vibes*

*Blissful Baths: 40 Rituals for
Self-Care and Relaxation*

***

AURA
ALCHEMY

Learn to Sense Energy Fields,
Interpret the Color Spectrum,
and Manifest Success

AMY LEIGH MERCREE

HAY
HOUSE

HAY HOUSE, INC.
Carlsbad, California • New York City
London • Sydney • New Delhi

Published in the United States by: Hay House, Inc.: www.hayhouse
.com® • *Published in Australia by:* Hay House Australia Pty. Ltd.: www
.hayhouse.com.au • *Published in the United Kingdom by:* Hay House
UK, Ltd.: www.hayhouse.co.uk • *Published in India by:* Hay House Publishers India: www.hayhouse.co.in

Project editor: Ashten Evans • *Cover design:* Shubhani Sarkar
Interior design: Karim J Garcia • *Interior photos/illustrations:* Shutterstock

**Cataloging-in-Publication Data
is on file at the Library of Congress**

Tradepaper ISBN: 978-1-4019-7632-3
E-book ISBN: 978-1-4019-7642-2
Audiobook ISBN: 978-1-4019-7643-9

10 9 8 7 6 5 4 3 2 1
1st edition, February 2024

Printed in the United States of America

This product uses papers sourced from responsibly managed forests.
For more information, see www.hayhouse.com.

This book is dedicated to the infinite continuum of spirit guides who inspire and support me, including my late medicine teacher, Laurie.

CONTENTS

AUTHOR'S NOTE

Dear radiant being,

My name is Amy, and it's been my job for 23 years to open the doors of consciousness and awareness for my students and clients. It's been my ultimate joy, and I'm so excited that I get to connect with you in this book. Together, we are going to dive deeply into the currents of energy and resonance that comprise our universe. We are going to feel and experience the interconnection between all things. And, ultimately, we are going to rediscover the love and universal life force that connects us all.

We are in this together! I hope that you have fun as we explore the amazing world of auras. This is not your grandmother's aura book. We're going to be diving into cutting-edge science and the most up-to-date, vivid, shamanic, healing experiences of auric energy that you've ever encountered. We will heal and optimize your aura to such an exemplary level that you can use your personal energetic power to manifest what you desire. You are the architect of your reality, and you can create it as you choose. Our understanding of the true essence of auras and in-depth knowledge of their mechanics is going to help transform you into a modern-day spiritual adept.

You don't need a guru because you are your own guru. When you learn to own your personal power through understanding and harnessing your aura and energy fields as well as those that surround you, a foundational confidence will sink into your being that you are responsible for your life. This sense of personal responsibility will be a revelation and a breath of fresh air as opposed to feeling like an overwhelming liability. You are going to have the indispensable knowledge that will enable you to take complete personal responsibility and take your life to heights you may have never believed were possible.

Mastery of consciousness and energy is the doorway to that. Understanding, repairing, healing, and supercharging your aura, which is not only all around you but woven through your entire physicality, will allow you to take these steps and more.

I have guided many thousands of people on this journey in myriad different ways through beginning to expert-level multidimensional shamanic work. I have written many books and worked with thousands of medical intuitive clients. I am 100 percent confident you can do this, and I am absolutely ecstatic to be with you on this journey.

I made you a special tool kit to support you in your auric learning quest. It has audio meditations from the book, playlists of music to cue up when you are clearing your aura and playlists for when we manifest our dream lives together using the auric particles. Plus, I've included color charts to reference when you are perceiving auras, audio mediations for each chakra to connect with their auric energies, and lots of other fun bonuses just for you! Get it at amyleighmercree.com/auraalchemyresources.

Your friend,
Amy
XO

INTRODUCTION

The Joy of Discovering
the Tiny Universe

When I was in grade school, my little brother and I used to play in the yard next to our house. We would turn on the tap attached to the side of house and allow fresh, clear water from the well on the property to flow out. (This was long before talk of water conservation was popular in our town!) It would gush forth with power and force, making an indentation in the warm-toned beige dirt and sand below. We were enamored with the water pressure, and I think we both enjoyed the kinesthetic sensations of the water and the sand on our hands and feet.

We began to craft a stream with branches and tributaries in that large side yard. It conveniently had a very gentle downward slope from the house to the forest line. We spent many afternoons and weekends there crafting the stream. We dug it into many forms, building on it and lining up our Star Wars figurines and G.I. Joes along the sides and in the towns we imagined lined the stream. We found layers of clay as we dug in the dirt and used it to form things. When snow and ice arrived, the stream would sleep, and when it melted, we would rebuild. It was the process that compelled us—the journey, not the destination. It was a sensory marvel that probably helped us develop wonderful dendritic connections from a neurological standpoint.

Early in the days of building the stream, when my hands were deep in the clay, sand, dirt, and water, digging and crafting, I began to see what I termed, in my mind, nature sparkles. They were tiny, white, and twinkling. They moved seemingly at random, and they seemed to gather and congregate around the stream and its edges. They became my friends.

I felt very comfortable and relaxed playing in the yard with my brother, and eventually the neighborhood kids and my cousins would come over and work on the stream with us. For me, the nature sparkles were frequent companions, especially when I was digging in the stream by myself. They felt innately good to me, and I didn't give it much more thought for many years.

Sometimes, when dusk was approaching and right before my mom called out to tell us come in for dinner, the nature sparkles would really intensify, and I'd see them everywhere. Not overwhelmingly, just sprinkled throughout the sky and in the yard.

When I would look up at the tree line, to the trees who felt like friends, I would see the trees' extended essences. It looked like a silhouette extending 10 to 20 feet above them in the dusky, darkening sky. It always seemed like the tree line was gently glowing. I knew the trees were alive just like we were, and I felt like it was their aliveness that made them glow. As time went by, I started to notice those glowing clouds of aliveness around other things, especially in nature. To this day, I still do.

It wasn't until I was in sixth grade that I began to think more deeply about the nature sparkles. I watched the movie *The Right Stuff* about the early years of the space program. The movie imparted a real-life experience had by astronaut John Glenn, who later became a senator. In one scene, he is in his space pod, orbiting Earth, and he sees golden-white sparkles all around the pod. He reported it back to NASA, describing it in detail. In the movie, they insinuated that they never knew what the sparkles were.

The scene in this movie struck me because it sounded just like what I would see in my yard, except it was around something hurtling through the edges of the upper atmosphere of our planet. I wrote a letter to Senator John Glenn. (This was back when we wrote letters instead of e-mails.) His office sent me back a large manila envelope full of information about his space mission and what they found out about that experience. It was a treasured possession of mine for many years

At this same time, I was studying chemistry and physics in school. Our textbook was entitled *Matter, Matter, Everywhere*. My sixth-grade science teacher, Mr. Buteau, was a witty and eccentric character who wore a white lab coat and inspired me to further love science. In that class, we learned about atoms being made of protons, neutrons, and electrons.

I began to consider if what I would see when we made the stream—we still did that, though I would soon grow old enough to lose interest—could have to do with these atomic particles. They captured my imagination in the same way that John Glenn's experience, astronomy, and black holes had.

I rarely talked about the nature sparkles that I saw. It wasn't because I didn't feel they would be accepted but because as a child I assumed everybody saw them. As I got older, I must've realized maybe they didn't. I didn't intentionally downplay it but didn't discuss it much. I would be surprised if I had mentioned it to my mother, but she would've been supportive if I had. When we studied that unit in sixth grade, I began to think of those sparkles as something I would see with my atomic vision.

I had always wondered what everything was made of and used to think about it a lot. But after that unit in school, and ever since, the question of what is happening with matter, energy, gravity, electrical fields, and beyond has captivated my imagination.

In this book, I want to share that imaginative and intellectual joy and the ecstatic epiphany of discovery with you. I want you to feel the happiness I feel when I indulge in thoughts about what everything is made of and experience aha moments, especially when I connect that with either my shamanic experiences or learning and intellectual understanding.

This "atomic vision" that I discovered as a child has served me for 23 years as a medical intuitive. I look inside people's bodies and find great joy in finding the root of imbalance and engineering a way to fix it. Sometimes this involves looking at the nucleus of a cell or the cell membranes and the way that they are or are not correctly charged due to the movement of their subatomic particles, including electrons.

I have taught shamanism for 23 years. I teach my expert-level students how to journey into the quantum universe and have shamanic experiences with numerous subatomic phenomena and then how to apply that knowledge to healing the body and understanding the true nature of consciousness.

I was fortunate to start my path with my medicine teacher at age 18 while I was in college. I've been able to combine my curiosity about the quantum mechanics of what is happening in our world with metaphysical expansion and the study of consciousness.

I am truly honored that you're reading these words and this book and want to undertake this journey with me. We are going to do our best to get a little bit closer to understanding what our auras are made of. We'll also even talk about whether there are subatomic particles and waves that not only carry our thoughts and create phenomena like telepathy but also are our thoughts. If the matter of our brain creates an idea out of itself and transmits it using photons, also known as electricity, and perhaps our consciousness is the fuel for this process, of what, on the tiniest most quantum level, are these phenomena comprised? Let's find out together.

HOW A MEDICAL INTUITIVE SEES AURAS

For the past 23 years, I have worked as a medical intuitive. I talk to people's spirit guides to convey information from them. I look at the energy of the body clairvoyantly down to a subatomic level at times. I look directly at cellular function, specific parts of organs, and inside the nucleus of cells and into the genetic structure. When I look at things from a medical intuitive perspective, I am looking at many different levels. I observe the physical level, meaning what the cells in the body and the molecules and atoms that comprise them are doing on the actual flesh-and-blood level. I'm also looking at the energetic level for what's happening in the body. For example, I may look at the organ meridian systems from traditional Chinese medicine and Taoist philosophy and the way that energy, as well as all the other electrical and electromagnetic energy in the body, interacts and creates our state of health.

The exciting thing about talking about those two seemingly separate levels of the body, physical and energetic, is that they are actually deeply interconnected. They don't just coexist; they are the same. An example would be when we were looking in someone's body at the lining of the lungs and the tissue there. Let's say that we were looking at the energy from a traditional Chinese medicine and medical intuitive standpoint and viewing the amount of yin fluid in the reserves of the energy contained therein. That's an important part of physical lung health and the energy of the lung channel meridian. The inside of the lungs are considered mucous membranes, and it's healthy for them to have a thin, damp coating of an optimal consistency there. That is part of the wei chi system in traditional Chinese medicine. *Wei* means "external," and so the external energy of the body is made manifest in that yin fluid lining of the lung tissue. We can see how if the lung meridian channel, having enough yin energy, would fuel the body's ability to create the right coating and therefore the right external chi, which is the wei energy, or the gatekeeper of allowing things in and out of the body. In that case, it would be a direct expression of the health of the immune system because if the lung tissue coating was optimal, then it would prevent certain pathogens from entering deeper into the body. This is a concrete example of how energy and physicality meet.

If we wanted to take that to a more quantum level, we could look at a singular cell in that lung tissue. We could observe the quality of the cell membrane and if it had the right ionized quality to allow it to retain electrolyte minerals that would help maintain that necessary, healthy coating. If we were to look at that one cell and then look even closer at the molecules that make up the outside of the cell membrane, we might see important ways to create greater balance. Next, we might look even closer at the atoms that make up those molecules, and can check their charge and behavior for health. From there, to observe clairvoyantly if the cell in question is correctly ionized, we would look even smaller!

We would scrutinize the electron cloud that surrounds the nucleus of one of those atoms. We want to see if that electron cloud is in the state where it is trading and sharing electrons, a process also known as *ionization*, with the other atoms' molecules in the cell membrane. Part of what might influence that is if it had the right fuel from an electrolyte standpoint. That could be anything from sodium to chloride to potassium to magnesium and more. Having the right electrolytes would mean it would have the right raw materials to trade and share electrons from those other atoms.

Here's where physicality and energy merge. Electrons, which are part of the physical matter of atoms, are made of pure energy. They are in fact one of the two main components of electricity. So, these electrons—which are so critical to ionization and to the body's immune function when we zoom out—are both physical and energetic. They are matter and energy simultaneously.

When I see the human body or animals, plants, the surface of the earth—anything alive—I see both matter and energy simultaneously. Every medical intuitive will likely be different. I see the human aura as a field around each person. It extends about three feet around the body in all directions. It sometimes has a defined edge, and sometimes it is more tapered. I view it as generally clear. I don't tend to prescribe to the whole color system much. In my view, aura colors change all the time and are mutable and fluid. I see the quality of movement, and because I have synesthesia, which means I sense something with one or more senses, especially intuitive information, I receive a cacophony of additional information. I do try to keep this turned off in day-to-day life as it's pretty overwhelming. I usually let it be on when I'm out in nature because it's kind of a fun array of sensory input. Synesthesia means that my senses mix, so I see a clear field around a human, also known as their aura. I know it's there. I mostly see the movements. I see the size. I see the quality. I feel the emotional energy. I feel the texture—usually multiple textures. I feel feelings, words, and states of being. In my case, I often feel health imbalances via the aura because I have honed that skill set for 23 years and devoted my life to looking at the remedy for imbalances.

I also feel elements of people's character. I tend to tune in to frequencies that are highly vibrational and essentially things that make me feel holistically good. Some of that, I think, often relates to personal preferences. As a sensitive type of person, I might be less inclined to feel a kinship with someone whose aura projects a lot of dark, dense, goth kind of energy. That doesn't mean I would not like them and doesn't mean I wouldn't get along with them. It just means that might not be something to which I would gravitate.

From someone's aura, I can usually feel the degree to which they're connected with the natural world. That could be because they're a gardening aficionado; it could also be because they connect with animals. I can see and sense when someone's aura isn't sealed properly or when it is well contained, which usually means the frequency is higher within it. I can sense some of their connections with their guides and nonphysical helpers. I may see their ancestors if they're close to the aura or electromagnetic field of the person. I can see when their nonphysical guide helpers' energy fields come close to theirs and interact and what happens.

For me, all this shows up as clear movement, kind of what it looks like when you see heat rising off the pavement and it's clear but moving. It's not exactly like that, but that's the closest analogy I could use to describe how it appears to me visually. A lot of what I see and sense comes also through my claircognitive senses, meaning I know it's there. I see it in my mind's eye, but I don't see it with my physical eyes. I do see the energetic movement with my physical eyes.

I also visually perceive a lot of energy and movement around plants. I tend to spend a lot of time in the forest. I've always visually seen the elemental spirits of nature since I was a child. Before I knew what they were, I used to refer to them in my own mind as nature sparkles. They would be present when I would dig in the yard outside, especially if there is flowing water involved. They would be present in the forests and at the beach and many places out in nature.

Later in the book, we will talk about the in-between times: dusk and dawn. And the in-between places, such as intersections of earth and sky and more. Those are the places where in traditional fairy lore we see more of the fairy folk. They are also the places and times that seem to be conducive to being able to see auras with your physical eyes. I tend to see more visuals at those times of day and in those places, and I certainly did as a child. For me now, it's more that when the switch is on, I see everything or a lot, and then to whatever degree I choose to turn the switch down or off, I see less. I just do that for my own comfort via my sensitivity level.

Everyone will experience auras differently, and we're going to dive into that in later chapters and look at all the ways that we have those experiences and what a tremendous gift it is that we do.

THE HISTORY OF AURAS

The idea of auras has enamored humankind for many centuries. Thousands of years ago, they were even discussed in ancient texts. From the discussion of energy in the human body in the Hindu Vedas of antiquity to the exploration of rivers of chi in the body in *The Inner Classic of the Yellow Emperor* and *Tao Te Ching*, which are part of the foundations of Taoism and traditional Chinese medicine, fields of the light have captured our imaginations for as long as we can remember.

The word *aura* has Latin and Greek origins and means "breeze" or "breath." The Greek goddess named Aura was known to govern breezes. The use of the word to describe a "subtle emanation around a person" came into vogue when used by the Theosophical Society. This group was founded in 1875 by Helena Blavatsky, William Quan Judge, Henry Steel Alcott, and others as a New Age religious movement. Theosophists popularized the term *aura* as well as concepts like chakras. Later public figures who were influenced by this group included Rudolf Steiner and Edgar Cayce.

Former-Catholic-bishop-turned-Theosophist Charles Webster Leadbeater became a disciple of Helena Blavatsky after leaving the church and wrote extensively about the concept of the aura. Blavatsky also wrote about the aura and wrote some of the books published by the Theosophical Society's press.

Edgar Cayce was known as the sleeping prophet. He was thought to have channeled volumes of information using his clairvoyant skills. Later in his career, he founded a spiritual center that is still in existence today. He wrote extensively about auras, including a book entitled *Auras: An Essay on the Meaning of Color*.

Philosopher, author, and Theosophist Rudolf Steiner, who also founded the educational system of Waldorf schools, wrote about auras as well. He penned a book entitled *Thought Forms and the Human Aura*. In the case of both Cayce and Steiner, there was a lot of emphasis on what auric colors symbolized. You'll notice in this book we do have information about that, but the overarching theme is that auras are constantly changing, so these colors are indicative of the present moment and subject to lots of interpretation by the observer.

In 1939, a Russian scientist named Semyon Kirlian made an accidental discovery. He noticed that when he connected an object to a source of voltage and set it on a photographic plate, it produced an image of a cloud around the object. After that discovery, Semyon and his wife, Valentina, set about to perfect the technology, famously applying it to a torn leaf and eventually to humans.

The torn leaf experiments cited as proof for Kirlian photography don't particularly hold up. Results were variable and are postulated to have been based on the moisture content of the leaf as it went through the drying process.

In some cases, the torn leaf placed upon the conductive surface showed a faint outline where the missing piece had been. This can be explained by stochastic (random) ionization and comparable effects, which basically means effects of various levels of humidity around the object or person being photographed as well as how grounded that object or person is from an electrical standpoint. Plus, the presence of potentially ionizing substances like bacteria, skin oil, sweat, moisture, condensation, and much more could cause this.

This type of photography is known as *corona discharge photography*. These specific moisture variants account for the majority of the visual feedback that comes through in this type of photograph. These variants plus the amount of voltage applied to the photographic plates and electrodes create the corona or aura in a photograph. For example, the scope and size of the streamers in the corona or proposed aura around the object in the photograph are actually an inverse function (which means a type of mathematical equation) of the level of resistance in the voltage circuit used in the configuration of the film electrodes. This means the amount of voltage applied affects the size of the proposed cloud around the image in the photograph so directly that physicists can calculate it based on the configuration of the equipment.

In the 80s, an opportunistic Silicon Valley dweller proficient in biofeedback set about to improve this concept and created something called the AuraCam. This is likely what you run into today at New Age and psychic fairs when someone is using an apparatus that claims to be able to photograph your aura. It uses biofeedback to read voltage and via electrically conductive plates, takes data and translates it into a color image that is superimposed over a standard photograph taken by the machine. The colors are determined by the program and the aura is not actually photographed. There's not much real science to back this one, and I'm sure it has created a lot of fun moments for lots of people over the years.

For this book, we are developing our intuitive senses of perception so we can delve into the particle physics and metaphysical and shamanic joy of perceiving auras.

JOURNEY INTO THE WORLD OF AURAS

There are myriad theories on auras. Some theories are rather constricting and claim that auras exist in a fixed, static state that adheres to specific colors. Other theories conjecture that auras are much more unconstrained and mutable. And then there are theories that fall somewhere in between. But what are these intriguing fields of energy that surround us, really?

In this book, we'll uncover the history and science and then dig into our own experiences and immerse ourselves in auric energy. Through this immersion, we will know and understand our own fields of light and resonance. That will expand our view to look at the world around us. We'll observe and connect with plants, animals, stones, and spirits of places to feel their energy fields and auras. We will learn to know on a deep level what energy flows through everything around us.

Then, we'll start to look at how that applies to other people in our lives, including the way that affects the quality of our interaction with our close family and friends as well as our experience of entering crowds. We can tap in to understanding why some of us may feel enlivened at a large-scale event full of hundreds or even thousands of people and some of us may feel ourselves shrinking and overwhelmed in such a crowd. We will look at what happens when many auras gather in a small space and what to do to keep our health and well-being functioning optimally

Next, we will explore what happens with auras during romantic intimacy and why the merging of our energy fields can feel so nourishing in the right circumstances and how to create and maximize that.

We'll deeply examine ourselves and our auras and learn to understand the incredible power behind the care, maintenance, and optimization of our energy fields. This care includes everything from cleaning and clearing the aura to filling it with energy to propel ourselves forward into the life of our dreams. That dream life already exists, and it is simply our task to merge our current auric field with the auric field of who we are in that desired reality.

Take your first steps on the path of understanding energy with me, and we will walk together with care and joy. Who would've thought that the understanding of auras, seemingly a fun and colorful pop culture concept, could be your doorway into harnessing your personal power and creating the life circumstances you desire? Life is full of surprises, and so is your aura.

PART I

UNDERSTANDING ENERGY FIELDS

Before we're ready to work with our auras, we first need to understand what they are and how they work. In this section, we will learn new concepts to better comprehend the anatomy of the aura.

There are quantum particles and waves that comprise auras, and on a deeper level, they relate to our actual physical bodies as well as our energy bodies. The two are beautifully connected. Our physical bodies are woven through with powerful energy that then comes out around us in electrical and magnetic fields. All living things have an electromagnetic field (which is a combination of two fields), and even some nonliving things have magnetic fields, depending on their makeup.

The study of auras is the doorway into understanding the nature of light. The amazing thing about light is that it can be broken down into waves and particles. Light waves behave like waves in the ocean moving through water, while soundwaves behave similarly to the theoretical waves in trigonometry and calculus. There is an intrinsic commonality to the behavior of light, waves, and more. Within the concept of light, particles move in ways that you'll see echoed in the larger macroscopic world.

We'll dive into not only the science behind auras but also their history and the different ways that humans have conceptualized them over time. With this knowledge, you can then form your own understanding. Ultimately, this book is about ideas and information, and I encourage you to integrate what resonates for you and leave the rest. Your understanding of reality is always going to be shaped by the lens of your own experience.

EVERYTHING IS ALIVE

Why do some people consider a human alive but not a stone? Why do some people consider the life of a plant to be less intrinsically valid then the life of an elephant? As humans, we seem to have a hierarchical scale of importance around this quality of being alive. But what does it really mean to be alive?

Is it the soul or spirit that we believe courses through the being? Or is it the energy? Let's say that being alive requires energy to be moving through something. For example, the energy that moves through our bodies animates our movement. Our somatic nervous system controls our voluntary movements. It's a biological process animated by the electricity that moves through the axion fibers of our nervous system and into our muscles. Is it the electricity moving through the body of a fish, telling its voluntary and involuntary biological processes to happen, that makes it officially alive? Is it the energy from the sun that the leaves of a plant capture and convert into fuel that keeps them alive? What makes the plant a living thing?

I ask these questions because as we think about auras, which are made of energy, we get to ask some interesting questions: Do all living, energetic things have an aura? Does having an aura indicate that something is truly alive?

If something has an aura, does it possess consciousness? What about rocks and minerals, which can have magnetic fields? Magnetic fields are a force, which means they do not have energy of their own. Does that disqualify them from aliveness?

We will dive into the scientific side of auric fields a little bit later. For now, I'll pose these questions and get you thinking about what it means to you personally to be alive. As a human being, what makes you feel alive? Obviously, there are exhilarating peak experience moments, like the time you went skydiving or zip-lined over a jungle forest. Perhaps the emotionally enlightening moments, like the times when you're cuddling with a pet or a loved one, when you feel love and connection.

I think it is an important thing to explore because one of the places we will land in our investigation of auras is that *everything* is alive. And this energy that courses through all living things may have a yet-to-be-understood defined quality. It may even be made of dark energy generated by dark matter, something that scientists have just begun to glimpse. It also has an intrinsically spiritual quality.

As human beings, we are inspired to seek meaning. We are wired to question and search. Because you're reading this book, that urge is active in you. You are seeking understanding and wanting to evolve. This desire could be built into your being by a spiritual energy of consciousness, or it could be built into your being by the nature of electricity and its movement through the human brain. Or perhaps both.

This conclusion that everything is alive and that everything is enlivened by energy is important because it returns to the fact that every piece of physical matter contains electrons as part of the atoms that make it up. Electricity (more specifically known as electrical charge) is constructed out of electrons and protons. This is different from electrical energy, or *electromagnetism,* which is made of photons. We'll talk more about these terms in later chapters.

Matter and energy are at least partially the same thing. That is why everything is alive. Whether it is matter or energy, it is alive. Matter is woven through with energy. The green grass and soil beneath that you may see out the window is made of matter and energy at the same time. The essential building blocks of that stuff are both matter and energy, which are almost always interwoven. The particles that comprise matter innately contain energy on an elemental level. Matter and energy are almost always engaged in a complex, intricate dance. Without energetic charge, the matter would collapse in on itself. Without matter to create a container of sorts for it, the energy would flash into infinite oblivion.

Part of what gives everything life may in fact be the tiny, fascinating, mysterious, and incredibly beautiful elementary particles known as electrons and photons.

EVERYTHING IS MADE OF THE SAME INTERCONNECTED BUILDING BLOCKS

To me, everything is alive. From the most massive of supernovas, to the breaching humpback whale, to the mountain range imbued with consciousness, to the blade of grass in your front lawn and the insect resting on it, to every molecule, atom, and particle. They are all living things to me.

I've always felt this way, and I never knew how to express it as a child. Years later, as an adult, I discovered that this idea is the same thing that the *Tao Te Ching*, a classic Chinese text dating back to the 4th century B.C., and the larger Taoist philosophy espouses. The *Tao Te Ching* roughly states, "All things flourish, But, each one returns to its root. This return to its root means tranquility. It is called returning to its destiny."

When I was a child, the tiny universe within everyday objects captured my imagination. I dreamed of the far reaches of deep space and distant black holes and supernovae and of what was inside the everyday matter with which I interacted. What was everything made of, *really*?

In our world, everything is made of something else, of smaller and smaller units of existence. Over the years, physicists have developed numerous theories to explain what these units are. They have employed complicated and wondrous mathematical functions and equations to prove these theories. They've commissioned and constructed huge particle accelerators to slam atoms together and see what shakes loose. An incredible amount of time and energy has been spent trying to figure out what is truly at the heart of all existence. Scientists and philosophers alike seek a grand unified theory that explains it all on every level, from the existential to the mathematical and everything in between. We are yet to find that perfect explanation, but we continue the search.

As a kid and adult, I always felt like a seeker of knowledge and new imaginative horizons. Sometimes in my work as a medical intuitive, I see myself as a mechanic of consciousness and energy, opening the door so the client can fix what ails them on all levels and reengineer the body and mind to optimum health.

The idea of mechanics just means motion. It is the movement and the motion of any system. Something called *quantum* simply refers to a small unit. Quantum mechanics is simply the motion of the tiny. Isn't it amazing to think about the fact that within everything we see, touch, feel, taste, smell, and breathe, there is an infinite symphony of tinier and tinier particles with which we're actually interacting?

All around you is matter, and it exists in three primary states: solid, liquid, and gas. Solid is the couch or chair upon which you're sitting. Liquid is the beverage that you are sipping. Gas is the air that you are breathing. An exciting and intriguing fourth state of matter is plasma. Plasma is the lightning that you see during a thunderstorm and the northern lights that enrapture your eyes.

All matter is made of molecules. I'm sure you've heard of H_2O, better known as water, a molecule that comprises about 70 percent of your body. The abbreviation H_2O indicates that there's two hydrogen atoms and one oxygen atom in a single water molecule in its pure state. Molecules are made up of atoms, and water molecules can exist as a solid, liquid, or gas.

When water is a solid, we experience it as an ice-skating rink upon which we can glide and spin. A solid state of matter, like ice, has a fixed shape and size. Solids are the most difficult to compress of all the states of matter. That's why when we lie on a bed, it might squish down a little bit but holds its shape. The atoms in the solid also consume the lowest amount of energy. These same atoms and molecules in the solid state are packed together the most tightly of all states. They are the densest.

When we take our skating rink and warm with the rays of the sun, the thermal energy that is applied begins to make the molecules and atoms move faster. They consume more energy. They melt and become liquid water. They still have volume and still take up space, and that water can fill whatever vessel it's contained within. But if the edges of the rink weren't there, it would spill out. It has no fixed shape. It doesn't hold its form. That's because the atoms and molecules within are spread out to a medium level of density. They still have volume, but they lose their form.

Next, if we take all the water that we melted from our ice-skating rink, put it in a big pan on a giant stove, and turn up the heat to high, we blast it with thermal energy. It begins to boil. It bubbles! It begins to change form and become a gas. That's because more energy in the form of heat is applied to the atoms, and they consume it and use it. The steam that's created is a gas. It lacks shape and volume. It simply floats away unless we contain it in something else. The molecules and atoms are the least dense in this state. They're the most spread out, and they can move freely anywhere. They can't be compressed and are the least dense because they are like free spirits!

Most of the time in our day-to-day lives, we encounter our strong, steady solids; our flowing, slinky liquids; and our footloose, fancy-free gases. Once in a while, we get the exhilarating privilege of witnessing naturally occurring matter in a plasma state. This occurs with phenomena like lightning. Plasma is like a gas in that it has no form or volume. However, it is so incredibly highly charged that it produces magnetic and electrical fields. It conducts electricity! Think about the air around you and feel how innately you understand it doesn't conduct electricity because it is a gas, and it is loose and not dense. It can't conduct electricity. Plasma can because it is so highly charged with kinetic energy.

Kinetic energy means energy and action. Sometimes we also talk about potential energy, which is stored, like when you pull back a rubber band or a slingshot. The force that will be unleashed when you release the tension is potential until you let go, and then it becomes kinetic. Then it's *in action*!

SMALLER AND SMALLER!

Now, let's imagine that we find a sun-drenched beach. As we walk along the sand, our feet make contact with the grains beneath. They're packed together tightly, and each piece of sand and the composite of the whole beach becomes a solid that holds us. The waves lap at our toes in their fluid form. Although the liquid has volume, its form is undulating and free. It is acted upon by the force of the moon's gravity that creates its tides.

We are breathing fresh, clean air and taking it into our bodies. It's a gas, and it is all around us, filling the space in the atmosphere. We come upon a party! Fun music is playing, and sound waves are coming out of speakers, traveling through the air, and reaching our ears. We see a beach ball is being used in a lively volleyball-style game and is being enjoyed by all. We look at the beach ball and begin to think about what is smaller and smaller all around us.

Imagine this beach ball. Let's use it to help us understand the amazing entities known as atoms that make up molecules. Our beach ball is made of plastic. There are many kinds of plastic, but at least some of the molecules contain carbon atoms.

Let's imagine one carbon atom as if it was our beach ball. Atoms are spherical and contain a nucleus. Let's hold this imaginary beach ball in our hands. Imagine a baseball suspended in the center of the inside of the beach ball. Inside this baseball, which is its nucleus, there are marbles: red ones and blue ones. The red ones are protons and the blue ones are neutrons. Imagine there are always six red marbles, or protons. In a pure carbon atom, there happens to be six neutrons, but in many other forms of carbon, there are different numbers of neutrons, so that is not a fixed number.

Inside the baseball, the marbles revolve around each other and bounce around but never quite touch, although they're infinitesimally close. Just around the edges of each marble, there's a little bit of a field so they bounce off each other's fields. They're dancing around in there, seemingly at random, at ultrafast speeds, having a blast.

Now, inside the rest of our beach ball, we have a lot of empty space, plus an electron cloud. A pure carbon atom contains six electrons. Our electron cloud is spaced out in shell layers. In our carbon atom, there are three shells, and each one contains two electrons. These particles are moving so fast that each whole shell, if we could see it, would appear solid. And these little electrons would be like tiny fruit flies in size compared to our beach ball. But, here's the thing about our beach ball: it's 160 feet in diameter! That's how big would have to be to explain the proportion of the electron cloud the nucleus.

Our carbon atom has an atomic number of six. That is because it contains six protons and six electrons in its pure form. When you think about the periodic table, that little number usually in the top left is the atomic number.

Carbon

EVEN SMALLER!

Let's be quantum detectives together! Let's ask some intriguing questions like: What makes up a proton? What about a neutron? What in the heck comprises an electron? Particle physicists have created something that they call the standard model. This model describes the elementary particles that make up those building blocks of not only matter in atoms but also energy. Physicists have used math equations and functions to describe and prove a lot of the details of the existence of these particles. There are some things that are still a mystery in quantum physics, and we'll talk about those a little bit later in the book. But right now, let's familiarize ourselves with the standard model. It's pretty cool! Here is a chart to show you all the particles/possibilities.

FERMIONS

Quarks

up	charm	top
down	strange	bottom

Leptons

electron	muon	tau
electron nuetrino	muon nuetrino	tau nuetrino

BOSONS

gluon	higgs
photon	
z bozon	
w bozon	

The Standard Model

Don't be intimidated. There are a lot of particles, but once I explain them, you'll get to see how incredibly enticing and invigorating it is to understand the tiny universe within and all around us. As we start to bring context to our world through understanding its quantum makeup, we begin to feel like we're a part of something much more intricate than we've ever realized.

According to the standard model, we have two categories of particles: fermions and bosons. All fermions have mass. Fermions consist of quarks and leptons. Protons and neutrons that exist on Earth naturally are made of up and down quarks. The four other types of quarks: charm, strange, top, and bottom exist in massive stars in deep space and can be created in experimental facilities like the Large Hadron Collider. It's named that because protons and neutrons are classified as hadrons. And what the Large Hadron Collider does is smash them together to liberate quarks and more.

The other type of fermion particles are leptons. Leptons consist of the infamous electron that we met in our beach ball metaphor as well as the muon and tau versions of the electron, which are larger, far more massive, and typically exist only in deep space and when created in a large collider.

The other kind of leptons that we have are the neutrinos. Neutrinos are the most zingy and quirky of the fermions. Neutrinos don't react with anything. They have a tiny amount of mass that is much smaller than most of the other particles that contain mass. Neutrinos fly through almost everything because they barely interact with any of it. The sun is constantly emitting neutrinos, and they are invisible to our eyes. The amazing thing about neutrinos is that over 400 billion of them fly through our bodies every single second without us even noticing! They are everywhere!

Bosons are a little bit more complicated. Gluons and photons have zero mass. You see photons in your everyday life as sunlight! Electrons absorb and emit photons. Photons are what we call light, which is optical energy. That is what our eyes register. So, when photons, also known as light, interact with the electron clouds of atoms, we see matter. Photons are the only things that we can directly see.

We can see light, also known as photons, when they are reflected to us through interaction with electrons and matter. Our eyes can see a narrow range of the color spectrum. We see only that which is reflected in that range. So, for something like the air we breathe, the light reflected off those molecules is not in the range that our optical system is wired to see; therefore, it appears invisible.

The W boson, Z boson, and Higgs boson all have mass. Particle physics theory states that something called the Higgs field was created in the instant after the big bang. An extensive and mathematically complicated theorem appears to prove that every particle that contains mass gains its mass from the Higgs field. The Higgs boson is a particle associated with the Higgs field.

The W and Z bosons are particles that are created through the process of radioactive decay. So, although they may exist on Earth, it's very rare, and we seldom interact with them in our daily lives.

The amazing and wonderful thing is that elementary particles are the building blocks of absolutely everything in the proven, known universe. The same particles at a fundamental level make up everything we see, hear, feel, smell, taste, attach, breathe, and interact with on a physical level.

We're also going to explore later in the book how some of these same particles may be involved in our spiritual experience. The photons that we see reflected and allow us to illuminate our world with sight are the same particles that flow through our muscle and nerve cells and animate our brains. Those photon particles allow us to have emotions and think thoughts. They make everything happen in our bodies. They interact with the matter and the energy in our beings and the world around us to create the entirety of our existence. This includes our auras! And, as we delve deeply into what truly comprises our universe, we will look within ourselves and find greater and greater understanding and look just outside of our physical bodies and witness the majesty of our auras. In this process, we will understand ourselves and our universe.

ANTIMATTER, ENERGY PARTICLES, AND WAVES

Let's talk a little bit more about elementary particles. I want to make sure you have a working understanding of some of them because we are going to use them later to manifest our dreams and desires through the power of our own auras.

The elementary particles that we discussed in the standard model are the basic framework. They have a couple additional interesting properties I want to mention just so you know that they exist.

The first is called intrinsic angular momentum; sometimes physicists refer to this as spin. This is not classical spin, like Earth spinning on its axis. It's a little bit more complicated and more aligned with its longer name of *angular momentum*. It is classified as up or down, and some scientists call it left or right. We don't need to think about this too much, but we may encounter the leader when we're manifesting using particles in our auras, and I want you to know it exists in case you sense it.

Another thing that differentiates specific elementary particles, meaning every quark, every electron, and so on, is type of charge. It's different than a positive or negative charge and a little bit more complicated. Physicists have classified these charges into three categories. They have names associated with colors, but they don't look like that color, so understand those are just labels. They're classified as red, blue, and green charge. The three charges have to do with the ways that particles can interact and combine. Another fun way to look at this kind of charge is to look at what scientists refer to as Feynman diagrams. Those were developed by Richard Feynman, who was a famous physicist, and other helpers. Those show the charges and the different ways they interact using triangles to help us understand which particles can interact with others.

Dark Matter, Dark Energy, and Antiparticles.

The thing that we want to put in our consciousness as we get ready to work with our auras later in the book is the idea that most types of particles have the possibility of what is called an antiparticle. This is another burgeoning area of study in physics, and I find it fascinating. Since I was a little girl, I have been captivated by the idea of dark matter. Now, the idea of dark energy is well known, and it is specifically talking about these antiparticles.

This idea of antiparticles has a metaphysical connotation to me. It's sort of like the metaphor of the other side of the looking glass. It's the flip side of everything. My late medicine teacher's teacher, Twyla, introduced me to that world shamanically through some of her writing. There was a realm that she referred to as *constant twilight*.

This constant twilight dimension or reality beckoned me. I journeyed there shamanically and found that which would be matter in our world was light and energy in that world and vice versa.

This is where I feel like I have experiences from a shamanic perspective with antimatter, including dark matter and dark energy. In this case, *dark* means the flip side, not ominous. This is where I meet antiparticles. I think there are a lot of interesting implications for us from the standpoint of energy healing and working with our auras.

The feeling in these realms for me is enchanted and high vibrational, but it also feels calming and like it opens the mind. I've intuitively observed in my brain that when I journey to those dimensional realms, I experience greater synchronization in my left and right brain. I feel like it fosters new dendritic connections because the hemispheres of the brain are working together well.

In my expert-level shamanic classes, I have students journey to that realm for that purpose. I like to take things in an experiential shamanic direction. Physicists developed the concept of these antiparticles to continue to explain complicated mathematical concepts and to be a part of different theories in physics like supersymmetry.

With the advent of high-level computers, physicists are able to run simulations where they do things like flip every left-spinning particle with every right-spinning particle and see how much of their theoretical and mathematical framework for the standard model holds up. That is the essence of the theory of supersymmetry in physics.

The exciting and intriguing new horizon of antiparticles is something we will play with later. I also want to make sure to call attention to the part of the standard model that shows you that every electron, muon, and tau has an electron neutrino, a muon neutrino, and a tau neutrino respectively. I want to remind you about neutrinos because I think they're intriguing, and we are going to talk about them quite a bit in later chapters. Remember that neutrinos are extra-tiny, but they do have a little bit of mass. This is why they are fermions and not bosons. We have many neutrinos generated by the sun flying at us all the time. We experience 400 billion neutrinos passing through our bodies every single second!

Here's the other thing that could totally blow our minds: antineutrinos exist. Where are they and what do they do? At the moment that's a mystery. But, they're out there, and perhaps we will sense them in our meditations and manifestation work in the final third of this book.

One of the neat things about elementary particles is that they are also, simultaneously, considered waves. There's a couple of meanings to this idea of the wave when we talk about subatomic particles. First, physicists assign a wave function, which is essentially a mathematical equation to everything, including every particle. That's how they mathematically prove the standard model and related elements of it, and in some cases they're able to verify these things using those particle accelerators and colliders that we talked about the previous chapter.

So, the question for people who are not mathematicians trying to understand physics kind of ends up being, are particles really waves? How can they be both? We're going to talk specifically about electrons and photons. The majority of what we are going to discuss will apply to most of the particles we talked about in the last chapter. But we're going to focus specifically on those two.

We're doing that for a couple reasons. The first reason is that they are very involved in our auras, and what we are building toward is alchemy and mastership of our own auras. The second reason is they are the nuts-and-bolts of energy and electricity. Electricity is a specific type of energy. And were going to talk about this in great detail;

it's all intertwined with our auras. We can categorize every-day energy into three main types: optical energy is light, thermal energy is heat, and acoustic energy is sound.

One of the most famous experiments in physics is called the double-slit experiment. It can be done with most particles but specifically with electrons and photons. Physicists tested it at the most elementary level with single electrons, and I've also seen a wonderful video created by a Ph.D.-level quantum computing physicist named Mithuna Yoganathan that explained it well. Her YouTube channel is called Looking Glass Universe and the video where she re-creates the experiment with lasers and a smoke machine is called *I Did the Double-Slit Experiment at Home.* I'd love for you to watch it because then you can see what I am going to describe to you.

The point of the double-slit experiment was to try to figure out whether elementary particles are waves or actual particles that are singular discrete units flying through space. The conclusion was they're both. This is especially pertinent for photons and electrons, and you'll see in the YouTube video, if you watch it, that the medium being manipulated is light, which is photons. In the double-slit experiment, whether it's a laser hurling millions if not more of photons at the apparatus or it's in a controlled physics laboratory where it's an electron gun or a photon gun sending a single stream of particles, the results are the same. The stream of light/photons or electrons is hurled toward (or shines toward) something that splits the beam in half. In the laboratory version, it's a panel with two slits cut in it (a double slit), so the space between them that is still the same panel is what splits the beam. In the YouTube video that I mentioned, Dr. Yoganathan uses a strand of hair and splits the beam of a laser in half.

When you have the strand of hair or the lab set up in place, then you spray the stream of particles or shine the beam of light straight ahead so it will land on the back wall. In the lab experiment, a sensor detects each particle landing.

In the lab, when you fire the particle gun without the panel in place, it is unimpeded and the particles land in a centralized spot, like you shined a beam and then it diffused out a little bit after. With a beam of light, it would be like if you shined a flashlight at a blank wall. There would be a circle with lightly diffused edges. In both cases, it lands where we'd expect it to land.

When you insert the piece of hair or the panel with two slits, something very different happens. This seemingly singular beam goes toward that interference item, and you can see its impact, whether it's with instruments in the lab or with a smoke machine in the dark, like with the YouTube video experiment. There is a pattern of waves coming through each side of the split beam, and they interfere with each other. You see the waves because of the interference and interaction between them.

It looks like if you did the same thing with water and were creating waves, and they went through these two openings. Two sets of waves came out. As they began to advance, they bump into each other. It looks like a pretty pattern of relatively concentric resonating partial circles that are a little bit smaller than a half of a circle. You'll be even better able to visualize it by watching the aforementioned video, and you can think about what it would look like if it was water to help envision what happens.

The beam is interfered with and becomes two forces of waves that we can perceive only because they interfere with each other. Otherwise, we would not see the waves.

In the double-slit experiment in the lab, when they all land on the backboard that senses where particles are, the particles are dispersed randomly and relatively evenly over the whole back wall. In the laser smoke machine version, we see a pattern of waves and light spread out over the back wall.

The piece of hair or the panel took the beam and bisected it, and we're witnessing the waves because otherwise, if the particles were not also waves, we would not see the interference pattern. If particles were not also waves, we would see on the backboard only a singular stream of light or particles split in half, and you would just see the shadow of whatever you put there. But that is not what happens! Instead, the wave action and the interference put the particles somewhere very different.

This is how physicists were able to prove that elementary particles are in fact particles and waves. If you remember, I mentioned that physicists create a wave function equation for every particle and every thing. This experiment tangibly proved that it isn't just an equation; it is real.

I have wished for most of my adult life that I was an innate high-level mathematician. As a child, I had lots of learning disabilities and did well in math because I had a propensity for it, but when I reached college and encountered calculus and calculus two, that all came to a grinding halt. Even so, the majesty and beauty of mathematics astounds me. I want to highlight this for you because it is a big part of physics, and it is an intrinsic part to the behavior of the particles and waves that comprise our auras.

Here's a majesty of mathematics moment: we talked about the position of the particles of the double-slit experiment when they landed on the back wall. The thing that's amazing about the math involved is that if we're talking about a single particle and trying to figure out where it will end up, whether it's in the double-slit experiment or elsewhere, physicists can take that wave function equation and then square it, which means multiply it by itself, to figure out the probability of where that particle will land. And this is verifiable and mathematically workable at such a level that it can boggle your mind, even if you only partially understand it. Sometimes physicists refer to elements of this math as calculating the probability of the superposition of a particle.

Our bodies are made of math. The arrangement of our particles and waves, and our consciousness, are all governed by incredibly beautiful mathematical equations. Which came first, the matter or the math? It's a good question. But the math is a system that can help us understand the universe. In this book, we won't do any math but will appreciate it, and when we work experientially in the third part of our book to manifest things using our auras, we may sense that math or its patterns. We may feel it, and I want you to have an appreciation of it, so when you do encounter it in your meditations, you can gaze upon its magnificence and appreciate the beauty and majesty of life.

FIELDS AND FORCES
OF EVERYTHING

Once we think about particles and understand that they are also waves, we can widen our view even further because these waves are not just linear and two-dimensional in nature. They are three-dimensional, meaning that they extend out in all directions at all times. They create a field. One way to think about particles, that physicists have math to substantiate, is that each particle is an excitation of its field.

In a shamanic journey with a guide known as Grandmother Sky Blanket, who is one of the seven grandmothers from the oral tradition passed down to me from my medicine teacher, I had an illuminating experience to help me understand this concept. If we think of elementary particles as infinite fields, we can picture them extending in all directions and that each of the many infinite trillions of particles are doing this. We can almost picture it like three-dimensional graph paper but much more densely packed. All dimensions go on forever in this medium, and you can feel when you experience shamanically how each tiny particle is innately interconnected to every other particle due to this matrix of connection points that extends into infinity.

It turns out that everything is part of a symphony of infinite fields: all the matter, all the energy, all the forces. These fields dance together. Our visualization from Grandmother Sky Blanket of the infinite fields creating graph paper is not static. It's in motion. Because these fields are made of waves that are moving, and particles are moving around all the time (unless their temperature is absolute zero on the Kelvin scale, in which case they stop).

Each particle is an excitation of their field that's made of waves. Everything—absolutely everything—in all universes and multiverses in duality that are composed of elementary particles is made of motion. Life is made of motion. The term *quantum mechanics* just means tiny motion. That is all it is: the tiny motion that fuels all existence.

THE FOUR FORCES OF QUANTUM MECHANICS

There are four general types of forces in quantum mechanics and sometimes we refer to these forces as *fields*. There are even more fields to talk about in the existence of life and all that is. We have the field associated with every particle and all the waves. We also have four fields that are really forces, and we'll explore them later in this chapter. Finally, we also have the fields around everything, which we will talk about more later on in the book.

The four forces in quantum mechanics are electromagnetic force, strong force, weak force, and the Higgs field, which was created in the moment after the big bang and permeates everything. The Higgs field gives mass to some fermions, including electrons and quarks.

Gluons are particles that carry the strong force. Not all particles interact with and carry that force. When quarks absorb or emit gluons, they change from one color charge to another, which drastically affects their behavior and ability to create new combinations.

The weak force and the electromagnetic force were both created by a single force that existed only in the first moments of the universe called the electroweak interaction. After the big bang, the universe cooled quickly. Electroweak symmetry occurred, splitting the electromagnetic force and the weak force apart. This event was also what created the Higgs field.

As we explore all these types of fields, I want to call your attention to certain fields and their behaviors. One field/force has some bearing on our auras and has some behavior that can help us understand our auras is the electromagnetic field.

There's a whole branch of physics just devoted to electromagnetic field theory. There are electrical engineers who devote their whole course of study to the movement and manipulation of electricity, which is intrinsically related to the electromagnetic field. Photons carry electromagnetic force.

One component of electromagnetic field theory is that this electromagnetic field we talk about is two fields that are related and behave singularly. There's an electric field and a magnetic field that are related to one another but technically separate. In lots of cases, physicists treat these two fields as one, and in some of our discussion, we're going to follow suit for the sake of simplicity.

I'm drawing your attention into this so you can start to think about fields of all kinds. The magnetic field is measurable and scientifically proven again and again to exist is around our planet. As such, we exist within it, and when we fly in airplanes or hot air balloons, we're moving up into and toward the edge of that magnetic field.

ELECTRICITY VERSUS ENERGY:
THERE IS A DIFFERENCE!

Photons comprise electrical energy. They are absorbed and emitted by electrons. Electrons are charge carriers. Electricity is electrical charge; it's made of electrons and photons. Electrical energy is electromagnetism and is composed of photons. That electromagnetism, which is made of photons, is what creates the electromagnetic field.

Electrical energy, made of photons, creates an electromagnetic field. The actual particles of electricity that flow within a wire are electrons and are different from the electromagnetic field. Electrons are made of matter because actual electricity is not technically energy; it is a major component of everyday matter because electrons are part of atoms that comprise matter.

The tiniest particle of energy in an electrical circuit is the photon that makes up electromagnetic energy. Electrons are not electromagnetic energy, and they don't individually carry that energy as they travel down a wire. The actual energy is the photons that flow through the electron medium; the electromagnetism is the energy.

If we were to make an electrical circuit, which would be a circle of uninsulated copper wire, the electrical energy doesn't flow inside that copper wire. It flows in the empty air that surrounds the wire. The medium of electricity (electrons and photons) flows through the wire, but the electromagnetic energy flows around the wire because it creates a field. That's electromagnetism in action. We don't have an elegant way to describe that electromagnetism is the energy and electricity is something different.

I want to familiarize you with these different types of fields in our existence because we're going to get up close and personal with our auric fields pretty soon, and there are similarities and interactions between all these fields and ours.

I did a shamanic journey to experience the electromagnetic field again. I've done it before, but I wanted to refresh my experience. As we know, and what I did experience, an electromagnetic field is made of photons. In the journey, I felt the sense that electromagnetic force fields sort of held things together comparable to the sensation of gravity.

Side note: gravity is one of the absolute weakest forces in the universe. That's why particle physicists have not been able to prove the existence of the particles, that are theoretically deemed gravitons, that comprise it. It's so weak that it's very hard to measure.

In the journey, I felt like the photons had a pull to them and that they were a sort of binding force around particles and maybe larger things like atoms and beyond. I sensed that they created a certain cohesion and a photonic pull for the electricity. This is surely theoretical and from my journey work, but I think there's something to be noticed about this because we are going to go deeply into what our auric fields are made of, and this photon pull action may be a big part of it.

AURAS ARE
QUANTUM MECHANICS
IN ACTION

During every millisecond, thousands or even tens of thousands of electrical impulses are moving through our bodies. It is electricity or light that flows through our brains, nervous systems, and muscle fibers; beats our hearts; and much more. These electrical currents make everything happen, from the automatic functions of the body like breathing, the movement of blood, and pulsing cerebrospinal fluid to conscious or voluntary functions like muscle movement, running, jumping, walking, thinking, creating, and more.

Every one of these things and thousands of others are the result of the movement of electricity through the human body. The elementary particles responsible for comprising this electricity or light are photons. Photons course through biological structures and enliven them in fauna.

Some scientists refer to these particular photons as biophotons, meaning photons that are active and intrinsic to the state of aliveness in animals, including humans.

They are part of our biological reality, and life would not exist without them.

When we think, like right now when I'm writing this paragraph, photons are moving in the brain. They are part of the creative process. In a way, they comprise the intangibility of a thought. Remember our study in contemplation of the dualistic nature of elementary particles: they are both particles and waves simultaneously.

I have a theory that all these particle/wave photons that comprise thoughts are creating additional thought waves. These thoughts are made of at least part of consciousness. And my theory is that they create waves that echo through our reality. We discussed in past chapters that every single elementary particle is also a wave, and in addition to being a particle and a wave simultaneously, each particle is also an excitation of an infinite field.

That means we're existing in this endless, undulating three-dimensional graph paper like the reality of intersecting and moving fields, waves, and particles. I believe our thoughts add *thought waves* to the mix. I think they're made of photons, which are particles, waves, infinite fields, and perhaps other things too. Later in this chapter, we will discuss the possibility of telepathy, particles, and consciousness particles and what that means. But, for the moment it will suffice to say they all could be wave-like resonances.

BIOFIELDS

Another term for the aura is a *biofield*. Some scientists who study or conjecture about the field of energy around human beings refer to it as a biofield. It's a fabulously descriptive term and is related to the extension of the biophotons coursing through the body. If these photons are indeed moving and flying through the body at all times, then it certainly stands to reason that they are generating a field.

Electromagnetic fields are made of photons. Electromagnetism is made of photons. Remember how in previous chapters we learned that photons are electrical energy? They are there also interacting with the atoms that comprise everything around us.

Let's talk about what those likely are and how that air, though technically separate from us, becomes part of our aura and how we can use our thought forms to potentially influence it. Let's assume that you're reading this paragraph indoors. If so, the air around you is likely made of the following ingredients, listed from most to least: nitrogen, oxygen, water vapor, argon, and carbon dioxide. This air is matter. That means that it is made of fermions. If you recall from earlier chapters, fermions are composed of leptons and quarks, which are the building blocks of atoms.

Although the air is technically separate from us, the biofield around us extends out through it. We can think of our biofield or aura as a composite of the electromagnetic fields of the currents of electrical energy and electricity inside our bodies. That composite of many numerous fields in the body can create another bigger field, like an egg- or oval-shaped bubble extending out around us about three feet in all directions.

It extends out through the air. So, the electricity made of bosons and specifically photons from our bodies that creates an electromagnetic field around us moves through the medium of air, which is made of matter around us. This is a case, like most cases in biological life, where electricity moves through fermions. Fermions are matter, including electrons. Electrons absorb and emit photons. I point this out because I want you to understand how our field, also known as our aura, is interacting with the space around us even though it might seem empty.

What else is happening in the seemingly empty space around us? Well, for one thing, it's being shot through with hundreds and thousands of infinite trillions of neutrinos every hour. Remember our fun quantification of neutrinos: that every single second, about 400 billion neutrinos pass through our bodies. So, if we think about the volume of space each body takes up and the three feet extension in each direction of the auric egg around it, that adds at least another body-sized area worth of neutrino action to the mix. So, we could roughly surmise a minimum of 400 billion neutrinos are coursing through each aura every single second.

Let's talk about neutrinos permeating us. What if we could give them a charge of sorts from our thought forms? The spirit guides with the which I journey into alternate reality on a regular basis have taught me the following: when life is moving in one direction, neutrinos that have been given a thought charge can change the direction of life. To me, that means that they can influence our human body and auras, plus our experience and movement through space and time. We're going to talk in the latter part of this book about how we can apply our thoughtform energy and intention to neutrinos to give them that charge.

There are also likely many other interesting elementary particles in many kinds of different forms moving through the space of our aura or electromagnetic biofield. If we were to group all the different types of particles moving through our auric egg, I'd give them an overarching name that we can use in this book. This will be for our purposes of understanding and manifestation. Let's call them aurons.

Aurons

Aurons is a catchall term coined by the author to describe all the elementary particles that exist in the space between the edge of the physical body and extending out around it for three feet in all directions. We call that space the *aura*, the *auric egg*, the *biofield*, and the *electromagnetic field* of the person.

The question then also becomes, do they stop being aurons when they exit our electromagnetic fields? Or do they continue in that capacity in some ways? When they exit our bubble, do they take a tiny piece of us with them? And is that one way we can harness and manifest through elementary particles? I believe the answer to those questions is yes. We will explore this more in later chapters.

Through communication with the Celtic goddess known as Nemetona, I learned the following about our auras. Power and sacred space *is* the moment. We can find the power in the moment. We can open it with attention and presence. It is the equivalent of tapping the nucleus of a standard atom, making contact with and affecting a hadron (proton or neutron). When scientists affect hadrons, large amounts of energy are released. Power and energy are synonymous not only scientifically but also metaphysically and spiritually. Our personal power is in the moment. Our electromagnetic field is an extension of our body. Being present to it and giving it attention helps us tap in to the power in the present moment.

Next, Nemetona invited me to journey into the core of a photon. As I did this, I felt they had almost no form whatsoever and were almost just made of all formless energy. As I looked into the photon with Nemetona, she showed me photons as equal to waves that were undulating without waveform edges, and they were almost but not quite undefined. Photons have no boundaries. They penetrate almost everything and move through it with neutrality, giving charge to those beings (who are particles) that accept it.

To Nemetona and me, all particles are alive, and they can be approached like beings with whom we can communicate, even though their innate consciousness is different from ours. The closest explanation to how I feel about elementary particles and their personification is way I feel when I communicate with elementals of the spirits of place or nature spirits. It's a different kind of consciousness. It's not like a person or an animal, and it's even different from how a plant feels, but it's alive and conscious nonetheless.

Later that week, I connected with the goddess spirit helper known as the Hindu deity Kali. She confirmed that the fields of any particles, thoughts, and beings can combine into larger composite fields. So, an example of that would be the larger composite field of humanity's thoughts that Carl Jung called the collective unconscious. Another example would be the composite field of a forest of plants and animals that you could feel if you were outside it, witnessing it and seeing its aura or its composite field. I used to see that as a child along the tree line in my yard and elsewhere.

I asked the goddess Kali what the human biofield or aura is made of. She showed me photons, open space, thoughts, feelings, fermions, bosons, and forces, and that human thought forms can give the particles direction. She said dimension-hopping with forces and particles can happen through that direction given by thought forms and that all this happens in the body, radiating out and extending through the aura.

As I talked to Kali, and collated that with my other notes, I concluded that our human aura is made of bosons. As you may recall, bosons are force- and charge-carrying particles and include photons. These bosons are interacting with the fermions around us, also known as matter, as well as other bosons around us. Our actual field is made of bosons. Our auras are fields made of bosons interacting with fermions and other bosons passing through and outside our fields as well as with other forces and interacting with the environment around us.

Part of the distinguishing factor between bosons and fermions is from a microscopic, physics-minded standpoint. Bosons can sort of collapse in on themselves as opposed to staying spaced out in the form that fermions do within atoms, like in layers of electron shells, for example. This is due to something called the Pauli exclusion principle in physics. This allows atoms to have a certain bulk or volume in a nonliteral sense of the words. We do not have to get into the semantics of that concept, but that is one of the distinguishing factors between these two types of particles.

INFINITE DIFFUSION FROM GRANDMOTHER SKY BLANKET

My medicine teacher, Laurie, was trained in an oral tradition by her medicine teacher, Twila. Twila was trained by a Native American from the southwestern United States in a tradition having the wisdom from seven grandmother spirits. One of those spirits is Grandmother Sky Blanket. By being initiated into that tradition, I got to meet that grandmother over 25 years ago, and she's been a wonderful spirit helper for me ever since.

In a shamanic journey with Grandmother Sky Blanket, I was shown an infinite interconnection of particles. The part of that I found especially notable is that she showed me an infinite diffusion of particles as opposed to an end or an edge. Grandmother Sky Blanket is associated with that which is above us when we are in the center of the medicine wheel. She stewards and is part of the atmosphere of Earth as well as the stars beyond.

She showed me the atmosphere of Earth. Earth is surrounded by a magnetic field and, of course, has atmosphere around it. Both are synonymous with Earth's aura. Grandmother Sky Blanket showed me the edge of Earth's magnetic field. She showed me an infinite diffusion of particles of magnetism and that there was not actually an edge, although from a measurement and human mind standpoint, we might perceive there is. What she showed me was an endless diffusion and dilution of the particles and their fields that stretched into infinity. And that this is part of the infinite interconnection between all beings that we can feel and tap in to with our hearts, minds, and souls in meditation and through spiritual contemplation.

This same diffusion occurs around an atom or a particle and its field surrounding it. Though science has not measured this field yet, I am conjecturing and have been shown that it does exist in some form. So, think of that same diffusion as not actually an edge where the particles stop occurring, but their fields diffuse into less and less, so they continue to extend out in all directions in infinity in smaller and smaller quantities, homogeneously distributed as a diffusion.

This same diffusion occurs around the human aura. We have the edge of our aura about three feet out around us that is relatively defined from an energetic standpoint. But, there are still tiny diffused particles that continue to extend out into infinity past the edge. We are united by those same diffused particles with everything that exists. This is another way of picturing and understanding the infinite field theory of wave functions for every subatomic particle and everything that exists. In our past chapters talking about particle physics, we discussed how every particle is an excitation of an infinite field, and every particle is also a wave not only mathematically through its equation/function but also potentially in reality as an excitation of a field that takes on a wave form.

I love the fact that physicists and mathematicians are able to assign beautiful wave function-based equations to all these particles and to most things that exist and put them together and have them work out. Kudos to those scientists and those mathematicians who are able to exist in that seemingly linear world of mathematics that becomes incredibly nonlinear when you extend it into mathematical equations of infinity.

JOURNEY INSIDE A PHOTON WITH THE GODDESS HECATE

I did lots of research for this book in the traditional senses of learning, reading, and gathering information to explain concepts and use those real-world pieces of information to describe my theoretical ideas.

I also did another kind of research with my spirit guides. Because I have taught shamanism for 23 years and worked as a medical intuitive talking to peoples' spirit guides, I certainly have an active and close relationship with many of my own. So, when I want to learn or understand something, especially if it intersects with the metaphysical, I outsource it to my spirit team. It's kind of like accessing a high-level think tank filled with some of the best minds in the genre. My spirit guides have been companions and advisers that have helped me create a joyful, successful, and enchanted life since I embarked on the path of working with them.

I wanted to seek to understand elementary particles at an even deeper level. The standard model encompasses what we've discussed, but it is likely that everything is made up of something smaller and smaller into infinity. I've always sought to understand how things work and what they're made of. That's why I was tremendously drawn to particle physics and chemistry even as a child. My dad is an intuitive and natural engineer, and part of that kind of thinking has extended into my desire to understand quantum mechanics.

I embarked upon a journey to understand the theoretical anatomy of a photon. I worked with the goddess Hecate on this. She's been a trusted nonphysical adviser for 28 years. She showed me that inside a photon there is something called arcs and blurbs. When looking inside a photon, I perceived that there's a field around the photon. The arcs generate the field around the photon. Arcs look like a rainbow shape but are a little bit flatter. Inside the arcs are blurbs. Blurbs are tiny units of charge, and they look kind of like a piece of popcorn. Hecate also showed me that an arc is an arc of charge, and the charge is not positive or negative. It is more comparable to magnetic but not quite. It has magnetism in an innate electrostatic manner.

In another journey, all the elementary particles felt nonattached and neutral. I looked inside a gluon (another type of boson) with Hecate. When looking at a gluon, there's a field around it. It looks yellowish and has an almost sulfur-like psychic smell. It had a field, and the outer edge felt sticky. Next, I looked at neutrinos, which have interested me for a long time. They felt zingy.

I journeyed to understand elementary particles because I wanted to feel and sense what we could do with them in our auras in the later parts of this book. I wanted to be able to share a visceral sense of some of these particles with you and bring them to life for you. I wanted you to get this imagery and the sensation of the particles in your mind and in your senses so that you can feel their essence and know our world even better. Information is powerful. Knowledge is indeed power and by using all our means and senses, from the more traditional to the more extrasensory, we can gather more information and increase our efficacy in creating our reality.

ANATOMY OF MY AURA WITH GRANDMOTHER PATH KEEPER

On another occasion, I journeyed with a grandmother from that seven-grandmother tradition, Grandmother Path

Keeper. She stewards that which is below us and helps guide our feet in our earth walk. She helps us stay on the path of integrity and right livelihood, walk our path, and embody our life's mission through taking the right direction for each person.

She took me on a journey to a place with valleys and canyons made of dark-orange rock. It was dry, and it felt very synonymous with her many journeys with me over 28 years, showing me the path on the good red road, as it's referred to in the tradition, which means the path of correct steps for each person.

She had me step outside myself and pause the movement of my own aura so we could look at its anatomy. From the outside, the aura looked like many concentric thin layers of particles almost touching. Layer after layer after layer. My aura had a lot of green on the top half and yellow in some of the layers.

Looking at it, I could see it was made of photons. I could see up by the head it was more tinged with golden and showed how the energy of the thoughts had a different quality. You could see it in that part of the aura and had how it rippled out. I wondered what these particles of thoughts or thought forms would be. Telepathy particles? There was a different quality to the upper torso area. It was airier. I saw more green light there too.

As I looked at the anatomy of my aura in that journey, it looked like the lower part of the body had a more grounded and rooted energy. Grandmother Path Keeper also detailed to me how your aura is your cloak of power and holds some of your power. That empowers you and your aura. That part of the journey reminded me of the one and only conversation I ever had with the late author and shaman Lynn Andrews. I had a reading with her within the last couple years of her life, and she told me that power is attracted to power, and it's a good idea to be invisible on purpose sometimes. When Grandmother Path Keeper talked about the aura at your cloak of power, I could feel and sense how you could use that with intention for invisibility if you wanted and how it holds some of your personal power. Later in the book, we will talk about ways to protect your aura and seal it so only positive energy can interact with you.

TELEPATHY AND CONSCIOUSNESS PARTICLES

Dean Raiden is a researcher with a Ph.D. in educational psychology and a master's in electrical engineering. He spent extensive time researching telepathy and telekinesis. He's known in the parapsychology field for conducting experiments to help quantify some of these phenomena. One of the questions I have that I posed to my guides is: Are there telepathy particles? And if so, of what are they comprised? My best guess from all the shamanic work I've done on the topic as well as research into the science, is that they are likely photons. And their emanations and infinite fields get directed in the brain through thoughts.

Another potential type of particle might be consciousness particles. These might comprise part of us that is eternal and has existed in multiple iterations beyond the physical. Perhaps even constituting the soul or the spirit. Are they particles? Are they waves? Are they fields? Are they all this and more? These eternal questions occur to philosophers, spiritualists, scientists, and seekers of all kinds.

TIME PARTICLES, GRAVITONS, AND THE MANY-WORLDS THEORY

The idea of time particles, particles that literally are the fabric of time, are flirted with in the theories of general and special relativity made famous by the involvement of Albert Einstein.

In this part of the dualistic universe called Earth, time is thought to flow in a linear motion moving forward. (That is not exactly how I view it in the shamanic world, by the way.) In particle physics, we have these general buckets of fermions, which are matter and energy, and the bosons, which are force carriers. Is there a boson time particle like that which carries the force that is the movement of time?

Gravity, thought to be one of the weakest forces because it can be overcome by many other forces in quantum physics, has been theorized by physicists to be made up of gravitons. Gravitons are thought to be gravity particles. They are still purely theoretical in nature because they have yet to be proven.

There's also a trend in physics that stems from a more nonreductive school of thought. One version of it is called Everett's many-worlds theory. This theory was originated by Hugh Everett, a physicist in the 1950s, who proved with complicated and elegant mathematical equations a possible existence of infinite parallel universes born every nanosecond.

The idea behind this is that as particles move through space, and likely time, they can go in infinite directions, and at each of those nanosecond points, infinite parallel universes are born that do not touch or interact with each other in any way. It sounds very abstract and is considered by some physicists to be incredibly logical, especially because it's one of the more mathematically provable ideas in physics at this time.

There's also is a theory of multiverses in physics that postulates that there are many self-contained universes in different regions of space/time. One of the reasons that some of these theories come into existence is when physicists try to merge the idea of the standard model of elementary particles with general and special relativity, which have to do with time. Some of the mathematics detailing these two branches of physics do not jibe. So, people like Hugh Everett tried to create a bridge and a way to make everything work out.

There are other concepts in quantum mechanics where the math works out better when you use Everett's many-worlds theory too. These include things like non-locality, which is essentially bilocation of particles; quantum entanglement, which is the way that particles that are at a great distance have an effect on one another; and the concept of quantum tunneling, which has to do with particles popping up elsewhere in space without following a linear path.

Regardless of where this all lands, and I suspect it will be an ever-evolving dance, the idea of nonreductive thinking is becoming increasingly intrinsic to understanding our world. It means exploring complex concepts with nonphysical properties like consciousness, free will, and the soul.

I want to close this chapter with the idea that infinite universes may have particles and forces in many infinite dimensions that we have yet to perceive or quantify. There is so much more than what we know. When you explore your own perceptions through the activities in this book, open your mind and expand your thinking, feel with your heart and your soul, and access the infinite parts of you so you can perceive even more than you ever have.

PART II

SEEING AURAS
EVERYWHERE

Let's talk about perceiving auras. How do we see them? How do we get the most information from our five senses and our intuitive senses to best interpret auras? Our extrasensory perception plays a critical role in helping us understand auras around ourselves and others. It's a very exciting experience to get a sense of energy fields around living things. I'm so happy that you will get to take this journey with me and open those multisenses so you can receive this valuable information. In this section, we'll cover how to optimize your intuitive abilities to observe auras, know what to look for, and eventually know what to do with that information. Let's dive in!

AURA OBSERVATION TECHNIQUES

A wonderful part of perceiving auras is being able to notice even more about people we encounter. When we look at other people's auras, it helps give us more information around our dealings with them as well as a deeper understanding of the people we care about. Imagine you were talking to your spouse and wanted to have a difficult conversation. If you could perceive the quality of their aura, you would have even more data around how to approach the topic and their mood, their energy level, and their receptivity to what you want to discuss.

Another scenario where observing someone's aura would be helpful is in negotiating salary at a job interview. Perhaps you're meeting someone for the first time. Having the ability to use your intuitive senses to gather information can give you an advantage when negotiating. You might see a tightness or constriction in a certain area of someone's aura. Perhaps you might perceive a sound or an emotion or texture that would inform you a little bit more about the person's current state of mind and heart. This could help tailor your strategy to negotiate for compensation that feels good to both of you. You can see how if there were subtle changes in the person's aura during the negotiation, it might give you even more information around what direction you might choose to guide the conversation toward next.

In a situation with several friends who are discussing something, you might begin to notice qualities of their aura and notice a sensation that you are able to perceive around real-time changes in their auras that might help you understand the way the conversation is going and the way the interaction is going. It might help you choose whether to stay in the situation or exit. Or, choose to take an action to elevate the frequency and vibration of the situation so everyone's auras become more highly vibrational and everyone's able to feel good in the situation.

There are endless opportunities to use the information and understanding that we can glean from observing other people's auras. It's such a gift to have additional extrasensory and intuitive information with which to navigate our lives.

AURA ETIQUETTE
AND INTEGRITY

It is fundamentally important that we always adhere to what my late medicine teacher, Laurie, used to refer to as universal natural law. That means helping all and harming none. Our intention must always be clear that everything that we do and everything that transpires in any of our intuitive pursuits is for the very highest good of all life. Helping all, harming none.

Additionally, there is a definite code of etiquette around looking at the auras and energy of others. This also applies to gathering intuitive information on others. It's not polite to be nosy. Just like it's not polite to try to listen through our walls to our neighbor's private conversations, it's also not polite to do the energetic equivalent of that to everyone we meet. It is better to take full responsibility for ourselves and generally look only with our intuitive senses at other people if they ask us.

Now, if you are in a situation where you want to gather information for a negotiation, you would want to do so in a way that would be professional. If you are in a setting with a friend, spouse, or family member you would want to be respectful and use care and consideration. You would want to go into the intuitive endeavor with positive intentions only for the very highest good of all life. A great rule is to consider things as if you were the other person or people. Would you object to the observation? Would you feel good about it?

Put yourself in the shoes of the other person or group first, and behave with care, empathy, and responsibility for being in complete integrity at all times. Your intuitive gifts are a privilege and should only be used to help and never harm or cause mischief.

It is out of integrity to use intuitive information and perceptions to influence people to do things that are not for the highest good. Focus on being in integrity and honoring other people and their free will. Always take the time to think that through and apply that to each situation.

HOW TO PERCEIVE OTHER PEOPLE'S AURAS

Perceiving other people's auras is a skill that you can strengthen with practice.

Practice looking at someone else's aura by asking someone in your life aligned with this concept if you could practice with them. You can also ask them if they want to learn too. Practicing with somebody you live with will give you an opportunity to observe the subject in different situations and times. Looking at people's auras can open the door to allowing your multilevel intuitive senses to glean information about them that might be related to the energy in their field. Remember, practice this with somebody with whom you have consent.

You can practice a little bit when you're out and about in public and do so respectfully. Think of it like when you people watch and admire somebody's outfit or sparkling personality. You would want that to be done respectfully if it was happening to you. Exercise the same respect and care with what you are putting out into the world. That applies for the energetic side of things as well.

You can do a casual and respectful level of aura viewing in public situations. You might notice differences in various types of locations. For example, the airport might prove to hold tighter, constricted, more stressed auras, whereas the beach at a vacation resort might be full of happy, relaxed frequencies.

OBSERVING AURAS ALL AROUND GUIDED MEDITATION

You can do this process unobtrusively in a public space or at home with others around, remembering to be in integrity and practice respect.

Utilize deep breathing and centering to move into a quiet space. Breathe deeply and slowly for several minutes and become present to yourself and your surroundings. Get centered and see if you can even bring yourself into a little bit of an altered state. Unfocus your eyes and let yourself be at ease. The more relaxed you are, the easier it will be.

Next, look at the person you are observing and then allow yourself to close your eyes a little bit and look through a narrowed gaze. Look around the edges of their body. With your relaxed gaze, notice anything outside that bodily edge. Do you perceive a field around it? A haze? A sense of movement or quality of fullness? Is there an edge to that field?

You might not see it with your physical eyes, and that may begin to happen more later after you practice. You might feel it; you might *know* the field is there. That is a form of claircognizance. You might sense it. You might see it in your mind but not with your actual visual eyes. Do you perceive a texture or sensation? Do you perceive the idea of colors? Or maybe you even see visual colors? Is the aura clear or cloudy?

Notice that there is a field around that living being. Perceive the outer edge of the field. What's within it? Is there movement? Allow yourself to observe that. If you're in a situation where it makes sense, you could even close your eyes for a moment and allow yourself to let the perceptions that want to come in, like an afterimage of that auric field, enter your mind.

Practice in different ways and with different people. Like I mentioned earlier, if somebody gives you consent and you live with them, you can do this at different times of day and notice how their vitality level effects things or other factors. If you do this outdoors, it may work better without sunglasses. But, you can also try it with sunglasses on and see how that changes things. Experiment and have fun with it.

I'll share the story of a medical intuitive client of mine who was having a session with me in person. She was new to the work and not someone who was in the healing profession in any way, but she had been having some psychic experiences. I was communicating with her and sharing a reading with her that was pretty detailed from her ancestral spirit guides as well as from the spirit guides that help me with medical intuitive work.

Suddenly, she said, "I have to interrupt you. This is so wild, but it looks like green light is flowing out of your hands and arms and all around you. What's going on?"

She was a little bit unnerved because she had never seen anything like that before. We were out in nature, in a grassy sunlit meadow shaded under a tree. Her ancestral spirits were talking about awakening her inner being, in that moment something clicked in. I believe her spirit guides boosted the ability for her to sense my auric energy. What she did not know was that my medical intuitive spirit helper partner is Archangel Raphael, and that being has emerald-green energy. That's who feeds me a lot of my medical intuitive information. She was seeing it flow through me. It was very interesting that is was so visible around my hands because I was speaking, but it must've been flowing through my heart center and out through the arms and hands.

This is an example of the way that people's spirit guides can magnify their intuitive senses. Sometimes that magnification serves the purpose of opening those senses more completely and then allowing intuitive experiences to be more frequent. If you would like to open yourself up to that possibility, you can repeat the following invocation aloud or in your mind at this time:

I ask that all that transpires in my intuitive work be for the very highest good of all life and in accordance with universal natural law, helping all and harming none. I ask my highest vibrational spirit family and spirit guides boost my intuitive senses. Please help me see, perceive, sense, and understand energies and auras. I would like to receive intuitive information to enhance my life and expand my conscious as well as create a life of joy and happiness. Thank you so much.

SEEING AURAS OF PLANTS, ANIMALS, AND ROCKS AND MINERALS

This book primarily talks about auras or biofields around human beings, but a wonderful side benefit is we can use some of that knowledge to understand auras around animals and plants. Fauna and flora are also enlivened by biophoton movement in their bodies, and the movement of those biophotons throughout the organism creates a composite field around it, just like in humans.

First, let's talk about animals. A great way to learn about the auras around animals is to notice it around pets. You can also start to open your senses to seeing the biofields around wild animals. Perhaps birds outside the window and even insects can offer interesting observation.

When we think about pets, we can hone in on their auras in a few different ways. With dogs, we can notice the aura at a distance and then move closer to the dog. In this case, our aura is interacting with their aura. When you pet a dog and move your hand through the aura leading up to making contact with the dog, you can open your senses there too and notice what comes up for you. In the next section, entitled Seeing, you will get more in-depth information on how to perceive other people's auras, and this will also apply to animals in some ways.

You could use a similar process as described above with cats and other mammals that have fur and are pets, such as rabbits, guinea pigs, hamsters, and so on. Any animal that enjoys being petted offers this kind of opportunity. Just like humans, of course, we always want all physical contact with animals to be 100 percent consensual. Being sure of that is a great opportunity to notice the aura as well as feel your emotional sensations that come in from the animal when you tune in to it and notice its behavior. Does the animal want to be petted? And in what way does it like? Most pet people are already attuned to the signals from their pets. You can add in the aura information and see how it enhances your understanding of the pet.

For pet birds and wild birds, you can look for the aura around the bird when it's at rest as well as when it's flying. When it's flying, if you tune in to the visual senses, you may see a little bit of an energetic auric trail, but it's usually very subtle and fleeting.

The aura of animals is usually proportional to their size and comparable to the size of the human aura in that proportion. You can notice a subtle aura around a dragonfly or a massive aura around a whale.

When I swam with humpback whales in the wild twice in the mid-2000s, the biofields around the whales in the water was interesting. The water appeared to magnify the fields because of its electrically conductive properties. Once I was in the water and in proximity to the whales, I could feel their auras very palpably. When each one came near me so my aura was essentially engulfed in theirs, it created a more intense feeling of interconnection that I think the water magnified. I also felt the strong and very high-vibrational aura of the whales had a role in that as well.

With the five different whales I swam with during those two encounters, I could feel how each one was unique, just like people. Each aura had some unique qualities.

With the two juvenile humpback whales I met, there were differences. One was very social and communicative, and the other had a more contemplative and almost introverted quality. The social whale's aura was more outstretched. He or she wanted to communicate with me. The whale vocalized in my direction and then faced me, swimming toward me. The sound was amplified in the water, and I could slightly feel the sound waves move through my body. That whale's aura was a jewel-toned turquoise in that moment. It shifted to have bursts of magenta and yellow gold but returned frequently to that bright turquoise. All the color sensations I felt had a very clear, bright, photonic quality to my inner vision.

The seemingly introverted juvenile whale may have been younger. I saw her or him in a different encounter. I felt she was likely a female. Her aura was more pale pink and had a more rich, lustrous countenance. It was less like light you could see through and more like a sparkling liquid but diffused out at the edges quite a bit. It had white sparkles in it that were very prominent.

The three adults I met were two females and one male. The females were in their mothering mode, so their auras were both showing a lot of strong interaction with their calves. Both held a maternal frequency to encompass the calf that felt energetically protective but also emotionally attuned to providing that kind of nurturance to the calf. Their auras were strongly connected to and encompassing the calves when they were near them. Both had a certain maternal neutrality that felt like the emotional frequency of unconditional love and the sense of purpose to keep the calves safe until they were launched into adulthood after the journey back to arctic waters in the spring was complete.

The one male with whom I swam was an escort for one of the females, and he was at a little bit more of a physical distance. His energy was present, his aura felt strong, and his purpose was very defined in his aura. If I was to translate what I sensed into the language of color, the edges of his aura had a more midnight-blue and sparkly quality. As I got closer into the body with my vision, there was more of a white emanation. That whale carried an essence of energetic purity and felt like he had a connection to a different dimension that would've been described by that sparkly midnight blue. It had a very crisp and refreshing countenance.

I have swum with many species of wild dolphins. Different dolphin species seem to have different qualities, and individual dolphins seem to have defined aura characteristics. The night before meeting a particular dolphin in the wild, I dreamed of that being. It felt like a male dolphin, and he showed up with an aura that was like orange-sherbet, rich and thick and iridescent. It was very high vibrational and filled with a lot of joyful and ecstatic energy, but it also contained the essence of a strong sensory presence component. I dreamed of that orange color and that dolphin but did not see the orange as an aura in the dream. It was more of a separate impression.

When I swam with him and met him in the wild, I was being slowly towed behind a boat, holding on to a rope in the Bahamas with my face and snorkel mask immersed in the water. He swam beneath me, and his orange aura was very apparent. He beamed it out around him, and there were also some yellow sparkle components. Our auras were in contact because he was swimming just about five feet below me, whirling and twirling. When he was farther away, I could sense the fullness of his aura. When he came a little bit closer, I could feel the interaction of our auras while both of us were in actual motion through the water. He was an Atlantic spotted dolphin. He and his friends were generally playful, although they all had diverse biofields and essences.

I swam with the bottlenose dolphins numerous times, and their essence overall felt a little bit calmer. Their individual auras and essences were variable as well. The same thing was the case with Hawaiian spinner dolphins, who displayed incredibly playful and acrobatic behavior in the wild and were sociable. They were very interested in human beings, who were in their wild environment off various beaches on various Hawaiian Islands. The spinner dolphins had a little bit more of an essence of group consciousness than the bottlenose dolphins; however, once again, their individual biofields were distinctive. I am an avid supporter of animal freedom and rights. I do not attend zoos or anywhere where animals are placed in captivity unless they are all rescues who are unable to live in the wild on their own.

As I'm sure you'll feel with all animals, whether wild or pets, when you tune in to them and their auras, it gives you a gateway into seeing their individuality. You can also observe different species and their similarities as well as their differences in terms of how their auras present and the way that collates to their behaviors and personalities. It can be especially useful if you have pets to understand and support your pets with this knowledge so they can live their most optimal lives.

When you notice the biofield around a plant, sometimes you have to tune in a little bit more deeply. These fields are typically a little bit subtler and more refined. When you look at a plant, especially one in the wild, unfocus your eyes. In that state, sometimes you can see the edges of its field with your physical eyes a few feet out from the branches. This works especially well with trees.

You might notice that the aura around plants is not quite as large in proportion to the plant's volume as we see with animals. That is not always the case, but it can be. Another good spot to look for auras is along a larger tree line, which is going to show you a composite biofield of the trees that are next to one another. That's a great way to begin seeing auras because those fields can be stronger and more noticeable.

Observing the edge of forests or groups of trees to see their auras is a good way to start noticing auras in general. Sometimes it is easier to see or sense these biofields at the "between times," dawn and dusk. As the sun is setting or rising, the light is a little more filtered, and sometimes auras appear more prominently. This is definitely the case for trees and groups of trees, sometimes for other plants, and even for animals and people. Experiment with those times of day using the techniques in the Seeing chapter in this book to take those perceptions to the next level.

As you know, auras are also called biofields. In the case of rocks and minerals, there is not a movement of photons through a living physical organism in the sense that we see in animals or plants. However, from a physics perspective, many minerals have magnetic properties. Some minerals are deemed ferromagnetic. That's because they have iron, nickel, and/or cobalt atoms within them in a large enough quantity to make them magnetic. These types of minerals include magnetite (also known as lodestones) and pyrrhotite. The element titanium is less magnetic than ferromagnetic substances but has some magnetism.

Igneous rock is formed via magma/lava. Magma is the lava within Earth, and once it erupts onto the surface, it's called lava. Both have a high iron content, which increases their magnetic field. Most meteorites contain iron, and so magnets will stick to them in some cases.

Does magnetism indicate electromagnetism? Magnetic and electric fields are related and together create the property known as electromagnetism. A moving electric charge generates a magnetic field. This magnetic field can create electric charge movement, which results in an electric field. They influence and interact with one another.

We can conjecture that magnetic stones have a strong field around them that is magnetic and electromagnetic in nature. This would certainly constitute a strong aura in our vernacular. But, what about other stones with weaker magnetic properties? Lots of people who consider themselves clairvoyant feel they are able to see or sense a field of energy around a rock or mineral. The current trending popularity of crystals may be partially due that idea.

My view is somewhat Taoist in nature, and that means that everything is alive. So, to some degree, it is imbued with a certain amount of neutral consciousness or metaphysical energy that does not necessarily indicate any kind of intelligent design but simply exists.

There are some rocks and minerals that feel especially sentient to intuitive people. It stands to reason that they would have what we would call an aura, where their consciousness is radiating out beyond the physical matter of the stone. The interconnection that we've talked about in previous chapters can also lean us in that direction. I have personally encountered large rocks and minerals out in nature that have felt like they contained consciousness, and I have seen a field of sorts around them. To me, it was a little bit different from what we feel and sense around people and plants.

Experiment with this for yourself. Use the processes in the Seeing chapter to tune in to your perceptions around various rocks and minerals and notice what you feel. Ultimately, intuition and perception of nonphysical phenomena is relatively subjective. What rings true and resonates for you might be different from what somebody else perceives. That's okay, and it's part of the beautiful diversity of humanity.

Do Places Have Auras?

In many of my advanced shamanism classes, I teach about how to work with the spirits of a geographic location. Some traditions call these spirits of place devas or elementals. These are beings of small- and large-scale that are over light areas. I tend to see them and sense them in wild nature, sometimes in residential areas, and, very occasionally, in urban areas. Sometimes, along with non-physical beings who help steward geographical locations, there can be a composite energy field surrounding the area. It's especially true in places like freestanding groves of trees, mountains, peninsulas, islands, smaller beaches, and other hills and promontories. They sometimes display fields around them. These are like the auras of a place. I think one of the reasons we can perceive auras in these places is because they are a little bit more defined. When they're more defined, we can sense a more finite composite energy field surrounding the areas.

Another notable field belongs to Earth herself. As we discussed in previous chapters, it has a magnetic field that has been scientifically measured. Earth also has its atmosphere. And it likely does have an energetic biofield of sorts that is a composite of the energy of Earth and the lifeforms on it. We could call that the aura of the planet.

Do Human-Made Things Have Auras?

What if something was made by humans? Does it have an aura? Does it have an energy around it? If it does have an energy around it like an electronic device, does that mean it has an aura? In my opinion, I would say no. We are defining auras as biofields generated by living things. We are extending our definition of living things and being a bit flexible with it to potentially include rocks, minerals, and places. But all of them are naturally generated.

This also poses the question: if something is a living thing that was created in a lab—whether through genetic engineering, cloning, or something comparable—does it have an aura? The answer is most likely. If it has biological processes, it would contain a biofield. The follow-up question to that is does that living thing have consciousness and to what degree does the consciousness enliven the aura? These are emerging questions as humanity continues to explore different aspects of potential technology. Another question that may emerge later is in terms of AI, which is also known as artificial intelligence. Do AI devices have auras? If at some point there's a lifelike artificially intelligent human-looking robot, would that have an aura? I would be inclined to say no, but we don't know yet. We haven't seen what will be created in the future to make that determination.

PART III

YOUR
INTUITIVE AURIC
ODYSSEY

In this section of the book, we will discuss what to do with the newfound knowledge gained from observing your aura and the auras of other people. We will start to decipher the clues between what you see and perceive in an aura and what it means. We'll look at some of the different elements of meaning from various systems, like Vedism and Taoism. And we will explore how that information can help you understand the knowledge that your intuition is providing you. It is such a quest to gain additional information about the world around you. As a medical intuitive, I know firsthand what a gift it is to obtain these additional insights. I have built a successful business and created a life that I enjoy through many factors that have been enhanced by the ability to gain intuitive and extrasensory information. This can help us make decisions and bring greater comprehension to the impact of our choices and actions before they occur. There are many practical decision-making skills that include logic and creating multiple flowcharts using various scenarios. We can make lists of pros and cons and all kinds of things that are helpful in fostering the critical thinking that helps us solve problems.

Additionally, when we add in intuitive and extrasensory information, we have more fuel and data to make those best decisions for our highest good. I am personally a big fan of collaboration over competition and everybody winning. However, if there are scenarios in life where there is a competitive edge to be had, all these logic and critical thinking, psychic, and intuitive skills provide an advantage. Why not use every advantage available to you? We can then pay this success forward by teaching and helping others to succeed and achieve their dreams.

WHAT TO DO WITH THE KNOWLEDGE

There are many ways that we can take the knowledge that we glean through tuning in to our aura and the auras of those around us and use it for our benefit and the benefit of humankind in some cases. When we clearly set our intention that everything that transpires in our lives is for the highest good of all life, which means helping all and harming none, we put some nice parameters in place that mean that we are only affecting things in an enhancing way for ourselves and others. And that's a great intention to adopt and believe in because, of course, as decent human beings, we would want that. From a spiritual perspective, there are many different types of beliefs throughout multiple philosophies that talk about reaping what we sow and understanding that what we put out in to the universe comes back to us. Of course, that's not the only reason to be a decent human being, but it is a great beginning around how to enhance life for all sentient beings.

Part of this is choosing consciousness. Choosing to perceive all and cultivate conscious awareness. One of the things that helps us to stay in proper alignment with what is for the highest good is self-reflection and self-awareness. Both are manifestations of choosing to elevate consciousness. Because we choose what might be called spiritual awareness and could just be called universal interconnection, we feel something in our being that feels divine or sacred or embodied or meaningful. This can be secular or something else.

One of things I love about Buddhism is that it is a philosophy, not a religion. Although it is counted among the world's religions, that is, in fact, a misnomer. This is a philosophy based on benevolent nonattachment and cultivating the eightfold path. These tenets provide a philosophical framework that serves as a wonderful guide to life and our behavior in general. These are some points to consider in the choices you make with what to do with the knowledge you gain through your intuitive study of auras. The eightfold path of Buddhism consists of right understanding, right thought, right speech, right action, right livelihood, right effort, right mindfulness, and right concentration.

Though Buddhist philosophy can be judged as a bit austere by some, when we look a little bit deeper, we can see that it sums up the philosophical stance of many shamanic traditions, including the one in which I was trained by my late medicine teacher: help all, harm none, and live according to that universal natural law.

So, as we explore all the things we can learn through our study of auras, we can keep these tenets in mind and apply them to our lives as well. And as we choose to live in alignment with the highest vibrational frequency, we will manifest that in our lives. Every time we make a high-vibrational choice, we raise our frequency. Every time we have a high-vibrational thought, we raise the vibration of our mind and body. Every time we feel a high-vibrational thing, we raise the frequency and quality of our emotional state.

In the upcoming sections, we are going to explore different ways of viewing auric information and what it means. This is what I've learned from my spirit guides in my experience as a medical intuitive. Some of it is based on Vedic philosophy and Taoist philosophy. And some of it is based on what I learned from my late medicine teacher and the oral tradition in which we were trained. Take what resonates and leave the rest. (In fact, that applies to the whole book.) This book is here to enhance your life and help all and harm none, and so it shall be.

A VEDIC PERSPECTIVE ON CHAKRAS AND COLOR MEANINGS

Sensing colors in the aura provides such a wonderfully descriptive set of intuitive information. There are a lot of different ways we can interpret it. First, we are going to look at Vedic philosophy and specifically the chakra system.

Most of the well-known Western chakra system that we hear about today, complete with rainbow colors, is the most recent iteration of myriad systems and theories of chakra energy centers originally based upon Vedic philosophy. Vedism is based on ancient texts known as the Vedas. These sacred Hindu texts date back to 1500 B.C.E.

Beginning 2,500 to 4,000 years ago with the Vedas, many people and systems have explained varying versions of the chakras. These have included chakras of diverse colors and from one to 144 chakras recorded in different Vedic and other texts.

After the longtime popularity of the Vedas and another well-known set of Vedic texts called the Upanishads, India's spiritual belief systems diversified and expanded. Then, in the Indian civilization at the time, Buddhism and Jainism grew in popularity and were based on foundations of Vedic philosophy. Buddhism and Jainism both encouraged personal development and included the chakras in that journey.

Later in history, the Theosophical Society, popularized a rainbow-colored, Westernized format. The Society was collectively very invested in popularizing beliefs around the number seven in many of their texts.

In 1927, a founding member of the Theosophical Society named Charles Leadbeater published the book *The Chakras*, which was based around a system of seven chakras. He aligned some of the information with the general yogic view of chakras based on elements of Vedism.

In this book, we will align with a slightly expanded system, including the seven well-known chakras, plus an earth star chakra located three feet below us at the base of the auric egg and potentially infinite upper chakras located above the head. Plus, we will recognize the minor chakras of the hands, feet, and many other joints. Notice in the chart below that many of the chakras correspond with endocrine glands in the body.

From a medical intuitive perspective, I see chakras as mutable and changeable. They are always in motion, just like the aura, and more diverse than a singular system can truly describe. However, the color meanings ascribed to them in the Western model are useful in our understanding of auras, especially since in our auras the colors are often moving and changing and may cluster and change around the chakra areas as well as other parts of the body.

CHAKRA	COLOR	LOCATION	ENDOCRINE GLANDS
EARTH STAR	Maroon, Brown, Black	3 Feet Below You	None
ROOT	Red	Base of Spine, Perineum	Adrenal
SACRAL	Orange	Navel, Lower Abdomen, Sacrum	Ovaries, Testes
SOLAR PLEXUS	Yellow	Solar Plexus, Middle Back	Pancreas
HEART	Green, Pink	Center of Chest, Upper Back	Thymus
THROAT	Blue	Throat, Neck, Jaw	Thyroid, Para-thyroid
BROW	Indigo	Forehead, Brain Center	Pineal, Pituitary
CROWN	Purple, White	Top of Head	Hypothalamus
UPPER	Silver, Gold, Other Colors	Above Head, All Around	Pituitary
MINOR	White, Silver, Gold, Clear, Other Colors	Hands, Feet, Knees, Elbows, Joints, Other	Some Exocrine Glands

Bonus Content Alert: Hop on to amyleighmercree.com /auraalchemyresources to get my favorite seven chakra audio meditations!

Earth Star Chakra—Maroon, Brown

This chakra is located three feet below you and is associated with earthly energies and stability. I think of it as the base of the auric egg shape. This chakra can also provide you with access to your soul's past incarnations. It fosters a sense of being one with the earth. Our health is most optimal when we are connected to the earth in a deep way. This helps us to receive and align with material success and resources.

Root Chakra—Red

This chakra is located at the base of your spine and is associated with being grounded and rooted in your body. It fuels your feelings of stability and security. It helps you to find a sense of security in the world. This chakra is how and why you feel protected on an energetic and somatic level.

Sacral Chakra—Orange

The sacral chakra is associated with creativity, sexuality, and reproduction. It is in the lower abdomen. When healthy, it encourages opening to new experiences and exploring new possibilities. It helps energetically digest and release dense energy and ancestral patterns.

Solar Plexus Chakra—Yellow

The solar plexus chakra is associated with self-confidence and strength. It fosters self-esteem when in optimal form. It is in the diaphragm area, lower than the sternum. It stimulates joy and happiness and governs our personal power.

Heart Chakra—Green, Pink

The heart chakra is in the center of your chest. It is connected to compassion and love. An open heart chakra allows you to express love. It includes the energies of self-love, love for others, and universal compassion.

Throat Chakra—Blue, Turquoise

The throat chakra is associated with communication and expression. It is in the middle of the throat and neck. When optimally oriented, this chakra promotes honesty and integrity. It is related to the ability to feel safe speaking your mind.

Brow—Indigo

The brow chakra is in the center of the forehead, between the eyebrows. It is associated with intuition, and I also see it as an energetic force that empowers elements of cognition. It helps us to use our psychic senses to solve problems and gather information.

Crown Chakra—Violet, White

The crown chakra is associated with enlightenment and cosmic energy. It is located at the top of your head, and a balanced crown chakra will create feelings of spiritual connection and well-being.

Soul Star Chakra—White, Silver, Gold, Clear, Iridescent, and Other Colors

The soul star chakra is associated with spiritual growth and enlightenment. It is located several feet above your head. It is one of your links to the interconnected universe. It opens you to communication from higher powers and cosmic forces.

A TAOIST
PERSPECTIVE ON
COLOR MEANINGS
AND QUALITIES

THE TAOIST FIVE ELEMENTS

Taoism has no founder or founding date. It is a philosophy that began as a merging of nature philosophy, animism, and shamanism. In about 600 B.C.E. Lao Tzu wrote the *Tao Te Ching*, the foundational text of Taoism. It is partially centered around five elements: wood, fire, earth, metal, and water, and each element has a color. These create an ever-renewing creative cycle, beginning with wood, which fuels fire. Fire creates earth in Taoism. Earth forges metal, and metal holds water. And the water becomes wood and starts over once again in the never-ending circle of the Tao.

Wood—Green

Wood is the springtime of the creative cycle. It is the beginning and is associated with the color green. It is an element of innocence, adventure, and new beginnings

Fire—Red

Wood fuels fire and is associated with summer and the color red. Its essence is lightness, brightness, and growth. The red heat of fire is all about expansion and enlivenment.

Earth—Yellow, Orange, Earth Tones

Fire creates earth. Earth is associated with the colors yellow, orange, and earth tones. The synonymous season is late summer. In the Tao, the earth element is about the interchange of all seasons. Late summer is considered a short season in Taoism that consists of the last month of summer. The earth element qualities are serenity, effortlessness, and dreamy.

Metal—Silver, Gray, White

Earth forges metal and is symbolized by gray, white, and silver. It is identified with the season of autumn. The metal element fosters organization and helps us create structure mentally and emotionally.

Water—Black, Purple, Blues

Metal holds water and is associated with black, purple, and shades of blue. Metal creates a structure for the unrestrained, unbounded, and undulating aspect of the water element. The water element is aligned with winter and the end of the Taoist creative cycle.

YIN AND YANG COLORS IN TRADITIONAL CHINESE MEDICINE (TCM)

In Taoism and traditional Chinese medicine—which is foundation of acupuncture, acupressure, and Chinese herbalism—yin and yang are loosely synonymous with feminine and masculine. The yin/yang symbol is a classic depiction of the balance inherent in the Tao. The Tao is balance and all that is.

You can think of it like this: left and right, up and down, heads and tails on a coin. You can't have one without the other. From a color standpoint, we think of yang as white and yin as black. Warm tones like red, orange, and yellow are thought of as yang. Cool tones like blue and purple are yin. Greens are a bit of both.

This information can be useful in the observation of auras for numerous reasons. Simply to notice the balance between the yin and yang in oneself or another as well as from the medical intuitive side of things helps assess the deficiency or excess of each polarity in the organ systems. This can be seen in the aura at times.

MORE COLOR
MEANINGS

The meaning of colors in auras are variable. It's about tuning in to how the proverbial supercomputer of your particular brain is translating the intuitive information that you're sensing. All the extrasensory and psychic information that we receive will be translated through the lens of our own experience. The clearer we can make the lens via our own objectivity and nonattachment, the more accurate we will be.

One of the tricks of the trade is to sense the colors and close your eyes and tune in to how they make you feel. Notice what they evoke. Is there a corresponding aroma or taste? Is there an emotion, thought, or word that comes to mind? Connect with how the colors you sense make you feel. Trust your gut instinct.

Below, I've included a table of some common colors and the meanings that I might ascribe to them in my work as a medical intuitive. These are just a starting point. They will give you some sense of what's possible as you continue your intuitive odyssey into the world of auras.

AMY'S MEDICAL INTUITIVE COLOR MEANINGS

Color Name	Color Description	Feeling	Meaning	Bodily or Aura Area
Apricot	Vibrant, juicy, rich, lighter orange	Joy, happiness	Sexual and sensual drive and feelings	Reproductive and endocrine systems
Aqua	Pastel blue with hints of green	Calmness, being in the flow of life	Psychic power, creative thinking	Neck, throat, kidneys
Black	True black	Solid groundedness or depression	Protection or negativity	Kidneys, feet, knees
Bronze	Metallic brown with vague hints of dark orange	Present in body and spirit	Leadership, high self-esteem	Area below feet
Carrot Orange	Slightly lighter than true orange	Contentment, well-being	Confidence	Abdomen and corresponding area in aura
Chartreuse	Pale yellow-green	Courage	Strong will centered in caring	Throat, upper torso, and back
Cinnamon	Red with hints of rust and orange color	Presence or anger	Feet on the ground in a healthy manner	Feet, legs, hips
Coral	Pink mixed with orange	Cheerfulness, happy love	Vibrancy of life, sensual and sensory enjoyment	Torso, whole aura
Crimson Red	Bright, true red	Vigor, anger, power	Ability to make waves in the world or rage	Lower body, throughout aura
Dandelion Yellow	Yellow with a very subtle hint of warm tone orange	Happiness, warmth, empowerment	Standing in one's power	Torso, throat in some cases
Denim Blue	The color of slightly worn, classic blue jeans	Balance, even-keeled temper	Trustworthiness	Throat, upper torso, and back; upper aura

More Color Meanings

Color Name	Color Description	Feeling	Meaning	Bodily or Aura Area
Emerald Green	Bright jewel-toned, rich green	Nurturance, caring	Healing power	Hands, arms, head, upper torso, and back
Forest Green	Darker green with a muted tone	Equanimity	Composure	Upper body, upper aura
Fuchsia	Vivid purple with tones of red to create an intense pink hue	Vibrancy, passion	Charisma	Whole aura, whole body
Gold	Metallic, lustrous yellow brown	Unconditional love, magnetism	Wealth, prosperity, nonattachment	Whole aura, whole body
Gray	Between black and white	Melancholy, listlessness	Sign of dense energy in aura or body	Whole aura, whole body
Indigo	Blue-violet	Clarity, knowing, decisiveness	Psychic and intuitive power	Head, neck, shoulders, and upper aura
Ivory White	Creamy white	Blissful, spiritual	Luxury, richness	Whole aura, whole body, above head
Lavender	Pale purple	Spiritual knowing, calm happiness, playfulness	Indicates light-heartedness and creative thinker	Upper aura, upper body
Lemon Yellow	Pale, bright yellow	Jubilance, upbeat feeling	Joyful disposition; likely energetically powerful	Whole aura, whole body
Lime Green	Bright, lighter green	Freshness, cheer, pleasure	Joviality	Torso, whole aura
Magenta	Rich pink, more purple than red	Enjoyment, innovation	Healthy indulgence	Whole aura, whole body
Maroon	Brownish crimson	Level headedness	Earth connection or blood stagnation from a TCM standpoint	Lower body, feet, whole body, or other areas if stagnation on the blood level (TCM)

Color Name	Color Description	Feeling	Meaning	Bodily or Aura Area
Mauve	Pastel purple with hints of pink	Inspiration, nurturance	Spiritual support from guides, divine feminine energy	Whole aura, whole body
Midnight Blue	Dark, sparkling almost navy blue	Determined, purposeful	Decisive, motivated; intelligence if bright and sparkly; yin energy blockage or stagnation if dull colored	If sparkly and in only upper aura and head, neck, throat then likely healthy. If whole body can indicate yin imbalance (TCM)
Mint Green	Pastel, bright green with hints of aqua	Lightness, clear heart communication	A gentle countenance, skilled at heart-centered sharing	Aura, upper body
Olive Green	Earth-toned green with hints of brown	Present, centered	Focused on the physical, practical	Lower body, upper half of legs
Orange	Half yellow and half red	Enthusiastic, jovial	Kinetic countenance, sensuality, passion	Lower body and aura
Orchid Pink	Brighter pastel pink with hints of purple	Enchanting, intoxicating, high vibrational	Romantic energy from the fairy realm, inspired creative energy	Upper body and whole aura
Pale Pink	Pastel, rose quartz colored pink	Nurturing, tender, gentle	Unconditional love and acceptance	Whole body, whole aura, upper torso
Peach	Pale pink mixed with orange	Inventive, caring	Artistry, excellence, genius, innovation	Whole body, whole aura
Periwinkle Purple	Medium bright, cool-toned purple mixed with light blue	Calm, inspired	Easy to channel spirit guides, communicating with elemental and angelic reams	Whole body, whole aura, neck, throat, head

Color Name	Color Description	Feeling	Meaning	Bodily or Aura Area
Pink	Bright, bubble-gum pink	Upbeat love, romance, frisky	Flirtatious, upbeat, playful	Upper body and whole aura
Plum	Red-toned, rich purple	High-vibrational passion, creative drive	Imaginative, charismatic, genius energy	Upper body and aura
Powder Blue	Pastel blue	Tranquility, relaxed	Serenity, integrity, diplomatic	Neck, throat, head, upper aura
Purple	Half red and half blue	Empowered, enchanted, bold	Inspiration, spirituality	Head, upper aura
Red	True red	Passionate, powerful	Material success, fame, recognition	Whole aura, lower body
Royal Blue	Bright, true blue	Certain, secure, dynamic	Honest, graceful, resourceful	Whole aura, upper body
Silver	Metallic, cool-toned light gray	Reflective, intelligent	Mystical, intuitive, sensitive	Whole body and aura
Steel Blue	Blue mixed with gray	Hardy, reliable, listening	Observant, thoughtful, resourceful	Whole body and aura
Tan	Pastel brown	Calm, grounded	Placid, sometimes can indicate health imbalance	Lower body and aura
Tangerine	Bright orange with a hint of yellow	Exuberant, impassioned, energetic	Present in body, sexual magnetism	Lower body and aura
Teal Blue	Bright, darker blue mixed with green	Kind, welcoming	Empathetic, tolerant	Whole body and aura
Terracotta Orange	Orange with a touch of red and beige	Tenacious, sometimes can indicate anger	Mature, hardy	Lower body and aura
Tomato Red	True red with a hint of orange	Vibrant, vivacious	Sensual magnetism, allure	Lower body and aura

Color Name	Color Description	Feeling	Meaning	Bodily or Aura Area
Turquoise	Lighter, bright blue mixed with aqua	Free, flexible	Open-minded, liberated	Whole body and aura
Violet	Slightly cool-toned vibrant purple	Inspired, genuine	Spiritually connected	Whole body and aura
White	Classic, bright white	Pure intentions, ultrahigh vibration, clarity	Angelic realm, connected to source energy	Whole body and aura
Yellow	Bright, true yellow	Alive, animated	Courageous, youthful at any age	Whole body and aura

LOOKING AT TEXTURE AND SPACING

As you continue to expand your skill to perceive auras, there are some interesting things to consider noticing when you are gathering information via auras or fields of energy around living things. One is texture. Texture refers to the way we would tactilely perceive something. Those same tactile sensations can be translated into energetic data. This means that when you notice and perceive an aura, you may discover that you are perceiving things in the way you would perceive the texture of surface. This could refer to the smoothness of chrome as opposed to the bumpiness of stucco. It could mean the slipperiness of peeled fruit as opposed to the dry texture of powdery flour.

We extrapolate the sensory input of texture into the aura through tuning in even more deeply to our sense of the auric field. This can apply to ourselves or others. When we connect to that energetic and aesthetic sense, we notice if things are sticky or parched in an aura, or perhaps they are full and have a plumpness that could signify lots of different things. Plumpness can communicate a well-hydrated body that is full of creative juice.

It could also signify the concept of damp accumulation in traditional Chinese medicine, and we get a sense of that texture in the aura. As a medical intuitive, sometimes I use information like that to help me go deeper into what's happening in the physical body. If the energy body outside the physical boundaries of the human being has a signature of dampness, that means that there is likely damp accumulation in one or more meridians in the body.

If someone's aura has a sticky quality somewhere in it, that's another medical intuitive clue for me to understand that there might be something comparable happening in the energy body. For example, if I feel a sticky quality in the aura behind somebody's middle back area, sometimes when I look deeper, I get to see what is sticky in the body. That could be a residue of plaque in the heart, inflamed mucosa in the lungs, or many other things.

Along with these applications of a medical intuitive nature, there are also emotional, mental, and spiritual components. For example, when someone's aura feels smooth and not staticky, that indicates that there's a good chance their nervous system is comparably well regulated.

That also tells us what's happening from a spiritual and energetic perspective because the overall energy of the human being often mirrors the energy of the nervous system. And both of those systems carry spiritual energy. So, when an aura feels smooth and even, it's likely that they're spiritually connected in one way or another, however they define it and even if they don't mentally define it. When you feel smoothness and a centered, well-balanced energy in an aura, it often also indicates that that is a prevalent emotional state in the person.

Next, we'll talk about the concept of spacing. It kind of relates to texture in a roundabout way. Spacing means when we perceive our aura, or, with permission, someone else's, we're able to tune in to the relative distance between the particles and sense how that feels. In essence, the question is, does it feel good? Do the particles feel like they have the right amount of space for their individual fields but also are close enough together to create a cohesive composite field of all the particles and essence of the human being? It is something that we feel into.

Use your intuition. It might be a feeling that is a fast sense of the truth, and it comes from your interconnection with all that exists. When you sense the spacing of particles in an aura, you want to feel a spacious joy and a sense of unconditional loving community between the particles. When we allow ourselves to imaginatively personify the particles, that helps us understand how they feel. Is their existence comfortable? Is the spacing that they are experiencing pleasant?

And, to go back to texture, is the texture pleasant? Is it enjoyable? These are some of the things that we tune in to and look at. Much like beauty is in the eye of the beholder, what feels energetically pleasant to some might be overstimulating or too mild for another. It is a subjective matter of preference to some degree.

As we will continue to discuss in future chapters, auras change all the time and so these textures and the spacing may shift and change. I've noticed over many years of observation that the spacing itself is an overall tendency in the person. There's usually an element of consistency because some people will be naturally a little more spacious in the aura, and some people will be a little bit tighter. A correlation I've seen from a medical intuitive standpoint is that people like me who have a little bit of hypermobility in our muscles, which has to do with collagen production, have auras that have more of that sense of spaciousness. Conversely, people like my friend Sienna, who have denser muscular makeups, also have denser auric makeups.

You can see that difference in personality tendencies within us as well. I tend to have a little bit more of a relaxed and easygoing personality, and Sienna tends to be a little bit more fiery and passionate in day-to-day life. I think we both feel some comparable levels of those qualities, but the way that we behave is perhaps influenced by many elements of our being, including the spacing of our energetic particles.

Now, that's not to say that we are defying laws of physics and the standard model around spacing and those mathematical computations. Perhaps this minute difference in the particle spacing in our being is more symbolic than literal. Or perhaps there is one infinitesimally small yet-to-be-measurable unit of space that is different between the spacing of our particles.

Most of these potential theories are conjecture at this time because with current available scientific equipment and experiments, we do not yet have the ability to measure things at this small of a level. However, humans are pretty resourceful. Fast-forward—whether it's 20 years, 50 years, or a couple hundred years—and we just might have it by then. That's the incredible thing about the never-ending upward spiral of evolution for humanity; it's unstoppable. Things that are theories now may be proven down the line, or perhaps our thinking will change and the theories will evolve into something even more fantastic.

MEDICAL INTUITIVE INSIGHTS ON TEXTURE AND SPACING IN THE AURA

In my work as a medical intuitive, I have noticed certain things about the texture and spacing of energetic particles in peoples' bodies and auras. Certain textures seem to indicate certain things in people's brains and in the aura in general. Especially in the aura around the head, having a static-like feeling energy from a texture standpoint can indicate energy that's not properly regulated. A lot of times its presence in the aura seems to indicate that there might be additional static coming from the nervous system, and we see that extended out into the field around the body. A lot of times certain neurotransmitter pathways exhibit a static quality, in my medical intuitive opinion. Sometimes, when people experience a lot of anxiety, they have some static along certain neurotransmitter pathways, especially GABA. If we look at the aura around the head and the upper part of the body, down to the shoulders, we can see some of that static around the body in the field. In that particular case, it's a good indication of the problem and an easy extrapolation to come to the remedy. That would be how would you ground that static out of the field and the body? How would you smooth it out? You'd ground it by going out in nature and placing your bare feet on dirt or grass, preferably in a natural environment that's not landscaped. That helps take the static and literally ground it into the earth.

Then, to smooth things out, it can be helpful to apply things that will calm the mind and calm the energy and the photons that the mind is directing in the form of thoughtforms. To do that, things like meditation can be helpful, and so can using certain herbs, with yin and calming qualities from a Chinese medicine standpoint.

If the texture of the aura is smooth and even, it's an indicator that the person is similarly inclined. If the texture of the aura is fiery and energetic, a similar conclusion can be reached. If the aura feels jagged or erratic, it is something to notice and take precautions in case the person's behavior or personality follow suit. Your intuition can help you line up with these insights.

The medical intuitive perspective around the spacing of particles is that a healthy amount of space is great. If particles are too spaced out, that can mean that the person isn't fully seated in their body and owning the space around them that is their biofield. If the particles are too tight and dense, that can mean that the person is attached to their incarnation. My opinion is that a balanced level of attachment is the one that will lead to the greatest amount of health.

To be successful and physically healthy and vital in the body, you do have to be present in it and in the space around it. A certain level of attachment can be healthy.

On the other hand, when someone is too attached to the physical and too emotionally attached and invested in things, situations, and even people in their lives, it can cause discord because the level of attachment is too strong. Then, sometimes the particles in the aura get more dense and may lead to the spacing being imbalanced.

The Buddhist concept of the middle way is likely the best and is indicative of the way we can view life, health, and incarnation in general. I'm a huge fan of nonattachment, and I think especially later in life when we are moving toward leaving the body, then we can go even more in that direction.

There are times from a medical intuitive perspective when we do see people who are tremendously nonattached to incarnation that have a hard time keeping the physical body vital. Obviously, in the case of ascetic monks who live in temples and monasteries, this doesn't seem to be the case because there is a vitality to their being and life-style. Perhaps their attachments to the structure and the philosophy are enough to give them a reason to live, cou-pled with a close connection with nature that breathes life into all.

That's what attachment is: the reason to live and be inclined to stay incarnated. So, the spacing of the parti-cles in the aura can give us a sense of where that stands for people and has a lot of medical intuitive implications around overall health and vitality.

Additionally, from a medical intuitive perspective, if there is particle overcrowding or undercrowding in a cer-tain part of the aura, that can indicate a physical man-ifestation that's happening inside the body. Sometimes physical ailments and diseases show up first in the biofield around the body before they land in the physical, so they can be cleared before they get there. Sometimes it goes the other direction, and the physicality is affected first and the echo is present in the aura.

SENSING QUALITIES OF ENERGY

In my work as a medical intuitive, one of the biggest takeaways I have is that every human is an incredibly unique individual. Of course, there are commonalities among people and medical intuition themes. But every-one is truly unique, like a snowflake. Just as no two snow-flakes are exactly alike, auras are also unique and no two human energy fields are exactly the same. The essence of it is no one person is exactly like another, even if they are identical twins or raised in the same environment. For each millisecond and even smaller during our existence, a complex series of decisions made by us and those around us ripple out, influencing much of our existence.

Does this begin in our quantum fields? Definitely. Does this mean that our interconnection with all reality influences the quantum fields that have created the particles in our bodies? Absolutely. So, when we look at qualities of energy in people's auras, including our own, we have an incredible privilege of tapping in to the diversity of existence.

So, in the endeavor to sense qualities of energy in auras and biofields, assets are openness and a lack of preconceived notions and expectations. We can use an open mind and heart to see, sense, and experience infinite qualities of energy.

We talked in this chapter earlier about some color meanings. We also talked about texture and spacing. We can also look at additional qualities in an aura. I'll include some examples in the table on the next page to get you started and correlate between potential states of being, emotions, and sensory input. You can tap in to infinite qualities by trusting your intuition.

Quality	What It Might Look Like	Potential Meaning
Sparkly, twinkling	Sparks in the air or moving, unstrung holiday lights	High-vibrational energy, angel and fairy/elemental energy
Glowing brightly	A brighter light than other auras you have seen	Lots of photons, powerful charge
Radiating extra far	A bigger-sized aura reaching out farther than 4 feet around the person	Reaching people, good communication, check for burnout
No discernable edge	A diffusion that seems to weakly keep going and fades outward for a lot of space around the person	Poor boundaries or low vitality and fatigue
Foggy	Blurred and clouded, not clear	Confusion, apathy, not following heart and best path, codependency
Smoky	Looks like puffs of denser energy in the aura; can be only in certain areas or moving	Can be a lower vibe and indicate use of flammable drugs, can also be indicative of ancestors who used fire in ritual
Dim	Faint glow and weak amount of light	Lower life force level

AURIC ENERGY IS WOVEN THROUGH THE BODY

The human body is made of matter, charge, and force, just like all existence in this universe. Sometimes we use the word *energy*. The fun thing about energy is that it is part of matter and is also sometimes used to describe what is more accurately known as *electrical charge* and *electromagnetic force*. The electrical energy, electrical charge, and light that moves through the human body is what animates it and gives it life. It's the battery that powers the whole organism! In spirituality, sometimes, we use the word *energy*, and it can refer to these things, plus the innate soul energy of our infinite beings.

As we discussed in previous chapters, the composite electromagnetic fields around all the electrically conductive parts of the body create a biofield around us. This is the field of electromagnetic charge that we sense when we look at auras. This extensively diverse field is as varied as all the many photons and particles of electrical energy and electrical charge that generated it.

We have the actual physical body, with its conductive material that includes muscle fibers, nerve fibers, cell membranes, and the fluid contained in various systems like blood, lymphatic fluid, cerebrospinal fluid, and much more. Additionally, after 23 years as a medical intuitive, I have seen and worked with the extensive Taoist meridian system, which has 12 major meridians that are like rivers of energy in the body and two additional similar currents of energy that are called vessels. Branching off from that, there are 361 classical acupuncture points throughout the body.

The various Vedic chakra systems have delineated anywhere from 1 to 144 chakras in the body. These are considered wheels of light that are connected by other streams of energy.

In all these cases, we have myriad energetic movement through complicated systems and vessels in the body, and all this then radiates out into the aura one way or another. The aura and its extensive composite of energy from the body is woven back in and through the body. The body and the aura are not separate. They are one organism.

An evocative echo of this body aura union that I've seen in my medical intuitive work begins in the body of each individual's biological, maternal grandmother. When your grandmother was pregnant with your mother, the eggs that your mother carried for her entire life, including the one that formed you, were present in the body. They may have picked up energies and frequencies from your grandmother.

The imprint of that egg was present on the inner edge of your mother's aura. Then, your mother carried you for somewhere between 8 and 10 months, and you existed inside her body and her aura, which had her mom's imprint on its inner core. Then she gave birth to you, and the imprint of the egg that made you, which was made by your mother and her grandmother, is present on the inner lining of the edge of your aura. This is the case for every human I have ever seen in my medical intuitive work.

What this means is all kinds of encoding and imprints from your mother are printed on the inside of your aura. You look out through this layer. From an energetic perspective, it colors the way that you see the world.

There are a lot of applications to this in my medical intuitive work. There are ancestral densities that are 100 percent congenital that we all hold. Unfortunately, humanity's history is pretty rough. The odds are some, if not many, of our ancestors experienced trauma and strife. In many cases, echoes of that get passed down, and this is one of the ways.

In my medical intuitive apprenticeship program, I teach students how to clear this themselves. It's something that comes up occasionally in my medical intuitive work. I'll describe how I do this for myself and with clients. You view the inside lining of the edge of the aura. If you recall in some of our previous chapters about particles, I shared the way that I see a sort of infinite particle diffusion on the edge the aura. I want to bring that up so you remember that even though we are calling it a defined edge to the aura, it does continue and extend out into the infinite web of creation through the interconnection of particles, waves, and their fields.

For our purposes, though, there is a point where that infinite diffusion has a distinctive edge, although there are still tendrils of particles extending beyond. So, what I do in the medical intuitive work to clear deep ancestral imprints, only if they are lower frequency and causing harm, is use my shamanic vision to view the inside of that auric egg. The way I perceive it is that the inside lining of the aura is imprinted with an infinite amount of coding. It usually appears to me in a language of sorts that is typically different for everybody. Since I don't know every cosmic family lineage language, my guides show me the frequencies and transfer the essences to me, and then we're able to read the lines of code, especially if were looking for something specific like the origin of a woman's deep ancestral fear of being harmed by men, or the origin of a man's inexplicable anger when he hears a certain tone of voice and experiences a certain interaction with another person, or the grief that is evoked in a nonbinary person when they encounter certain situations. These emotions may be beyond the experience the person has had in this world because we discover what happened to ancestors in the past.

When looking on the inside and reading this encoded information, I am often guided by my medical intuitive partner, Archangel Raphael, and we clean it off. Sometimes we use an eraser, or sometimes we have to scrub it. In some cases, it appears etched in, so we have to buff it off. We remove the code that has a lower-vibrational frequency then the person desires to embody. Then we fill it with a very high-vibrational code that is usually pure white light infused with joy.

Joy is the highest vibration in the known universe from a medical intuitive perspective, and so in my work, we use it a lot to bring everything up to its absolute highest frequency possible in the body and the aura. In our guided meditation chapters later in the book, I will take you through this exact healing so you can do it for yourself in a way similar to how I teach my medical intuitive apprenticeship students. This is one of the many ways that you can clear ancestral density from your body and your being forever. And, in this case, it starts with the aura.

This is an example of how that which is within the body projects outward into the aura, which is our intermediary, that then projects outward into our world. We are human projectors. We create our realities. Our auras are part of us and part of that process.

In the Gnostic traditions, there is a concept that I kind of like. I don't look at the religious side of things, but there's a concept of something called the great beyond, which is considered to be the void or emptiness, and something else called the great diversity, which is all existence. I think of it as duality. Between the great beyond and the great diversity is something called the Sophia. It's the matrix that connects the two, and it has different connotations in all the various triple goddess and trinity-based religious traditions.

I see the Sophia as an intermediate substance that translates the great beyond's emptiness. During the moments when the great beyond reflects upon itself, it sends out creation energy that travels through this matrix of the Sophia. You can imagine it as the most cosmically primordial incubator of creative essences where spirit somehow transforms into matter. And that is how the great diversity continues to be created through this intermediate matrix of primordial cosmic energy.

I think of the human aura like the Sophia between us and our interaction with the universe. We are the creators, and, in our case, we are fullness (not emptiness) in many ways. Within our fullness, our inner witness sits in complete emptiness, leaning back inside us and witnessing our experience. The combination of these parts of ourselves and more filters out through the intermediary matrix of our aura that contains the composite vibration of all of it and projects outward into our lives, creating our world.

AURAS ARE MUTABLE AND CONSTANTLY CHANGING

Just as every human being and aura is totally diverse, so is every moment of each person's life. That is one of the reasons that our auras are always changing. They rarely stay the same because our energy is moving at all times. As we learned earlier in the book, the essence of life is motion: general particle motion, wave motion, motion of photons, and overall energetic motion as informed by fermions.

In this constantly moving symphony of existence, the human being is an interconnected, undulating entity. We are constantly experiencing an infinite number of infinite particle fields intersecting our bodies as well as energetic movement in our meridians, chakras, and our energy channels. All this intrinsic motion in our physical body extends out into our aura. And, as we know, our aura is a composite reflection of our body. Our entire energy field, which includes the energy in our body and our aura, is a composite of our energetic blueprint in each moment. It's constantly changing because everything around us is constantly moving.

NOTICING CHANGES IN THE AURA

In our study and observation of auras in general, including our own, it can be valuable to notice changes. You can do this in several ways. You can notice it moment-to-moment throughout the day. You can also notice that when you meet up with people repeatedly throughout your life that perhaps you don't see on a daily basis. You can make a mental note of how the aura might appear each time and notice differences.

If you would like to get even more precise about it, you could add a bit more structure and do the following exercise.

Aura Observation Journaling Practice

Use a notebook or journal. You might decide to dedicate one specifically to your study of auras.

Choose the subject. Perhaps begin with yourself. After you complete your first round of observation, you can switch to someone else, maybe somebody in your family or a friend who ideally has consented to your practice.

In your journal, label the number of days you would like to observe the aura, giving each day one page. Ten days is a great amount of time, but even 30, 60, or 90 can work wonderfully. It depends upon what resonates for you.

After you've written the days on each page, you can put a few more fields to fill in spaced out over the page. I suggest colors, textures, spacing, emotions, other impressions, time of day (if variable). You can add any other ideas. You might also leave some space for notes. If possible, it can also be valuable to leave some room where you note what was happening in the person's life on that day. You might entitle that Daily Happenings. Obviously, if the subject is yourself, that part can be a little bit easier.

If you're doing this on yourself, you can choose the time of day to observe regularly, like first thing in the morning when you're brushing your teeth. If you're doing this with somebody else, then this can be modified. If they live in the same home as you and you always see them at dinner, then that would be a convenient time. If they do not, then it might be a different duration. Perhaps you see them weekly, and so you might label your pages weeks one through six or whatever will be convenient and work. If the schedule is not regular, when you see the person and are able to observe their aura, you could still label the days in numerical order but put the date. So perhaps day one would occur on April 2, and day two of observation might not occur until April 10.

Fill in the various fields on the various days and look back afterward, noticing what changed and what didn't. Notice correlations and impressions. Notice life events and their influence too. It can be illuminating to record observations like this and notice what changes when. If you're looking at this for yourself and you are a woman who is cycling monthly, you may also see some specific trends that relate to that. Time of day is also something of which to take note. I find for myself that's a big influence on how my overall biofield and aura fluctuates.

After you've completed your observation period and gone through and found trends, similarities, and differences, it might be fun to write a little endnote after all the pages where you summarize what you learned.

WHY AURAS CHANGE COLOR IN CERTAIN PEOPLE MORE THAN OTHERS

A lot of factors influence the mutability of people's auras. It's not just the frequency of that mutability but also the various categories that change and how flexible they are. Changes in color can indicate flexibility and mood changes. It can also indicate a certain level of volatility.

Some people are very centered, steady, and consistent, and there are some whose emotions and states of being move and change more. Neither is better or worse. But changes in color that you notice moment-to-moment or over the span of a few minutes can indicate changes in emotion and a fast-moving mind and sometimes strong emotions and volatility. Something to observe is that when you notice someone's (or your own) color signatures are moving and changing, it means that they are likely experiencing changing tides within their being. For some people, a changing tide is disruptive or rare, and for some of us it's almost constant. It's an interesting thing to observe either way.

From the medical intuitive perspective, I noticed that certain constitutions, defined from a Taoist and traditional Chinese medicine perspective, tend to be more or less static as far as how the aura behaves and how it is influenced by the meridians and energy channels in the body.

There are five primary constitution-influencing forces available for each of us from the Taoist perspective. They correspond to the five elements in that system. Most people have at least a combination of two elements that comprise the majority of their constitutional essence. The table on the following pages gives you a little bit of an idea. You can see in one of the fields the varying degrees of mutability in the aura based on these Taoist concepts.

Element	Organs	Colors	Emotions and Qualities	Aura Mutability	Aura Tendencies
Wood	Liver and gall-bladder	Green	Anger, sadness, adventur-ousness, excitement, impatience, exuberance, gluttony, rebirth	Wood element folks tend to have highly mutable auras.	This aura tends to be strong with high energy, and when out of balance, it tends toward excess. When balanced, innocence, wonder, and enthusiasm fill the being and aura.
Fire	Heart/mind and small intestine	Red	Joy, laughing, movement, growth, strong opinions, domineering, assertive, forceful	The fire element is just as it sounds: fiery. These auras are highly change-able and high energy.	The particles in the aura are often densely packed and active with lots of movement and proverbial heat to burn off. These people are forces of nature!
Earth	Spleen/pancreas and stomach	Yellow, orange, earth tones	Anxiety, worry, stability, planted in one place, grounded, resistant to change, deep roots, family oriented	Earth element auras are calmer and more fixed. They tend toward consistency and flow in more predictable patterns.	These auras can get a bit foggy with the echo of damp accumulation in the body. Earth folks are often suppressing the release of latency, which incites change. If they allow it, transformation is very healing for them.

Element	Organs	Colors	Emotions and Qualities	Aura Mutability	Aura Tendencies
Metal	Lungs and large intestine	White, gray, silver	Sensitivity, intuition, grief associated with lung channel, and metal in excess creates rigidity; empaths tend to be high with metal element	The metal-influenced aura can be light and ethereal. It is mutable due to outside influences and so requires fortification to hold its own individual energetic essence. Can become constricted if trying to control things in life.	Most empaths have a metal constitution as their primary influence. Sometimes, thorough evolution, they move into another element as their primary (often water). This occurs when they inhabit their being and are able to manage sensitivity levels. They tend to be psychic and sense auras easily as long as fortified.
Water	Kidneys and bladder	Black, blue	Charismatic, successful, magnetic, can be fearful, leaders, nonconformist, can be extreme; important to prioritize integrity so not swayed to bend important rules; needs to bring conscious awareness to avoid hoarding power	Others want to be in their aura and gravitate there. The water element is less sensitive and so is less affected by other auras. This aura is strong and individualized, able to own their space and hold their own essence in the aura well, so they have lower mutability.	Aura tends to hold charismatic energy and so attracts people, tends to have a strong presence and powerful aura. They still change if they want, but they call the shots more strongly in the aura as opposed to bodily forces and flow. Their aura does what they want unless they are ill.

USING AURA
KNOWLEDGE IN THE
EVERYDAY WORLD

Now you have a plethora of knowledge about what all the impressions that you may receive about your aura or someone else's could mean, how in the world do you sort it all out? One word: practice! It takes time to see patterns and tendencies in yourself and others and refine your senses. It also takes learning and knowledge, which you are currently gaining at a rapid pace.

One of the key ingredients is introspection. Contemplating the lens of your experience can help you translate influences that your mind and your life experience places on the intuitive information you receive. And your lens is valuable, by the way. We do not want to necessarily minimize it, but we want to see it for what it is.

The more we self-reflect, the more we understand what's happening within. Because we are human projectors, we create our realities. That which is within us manifests in our life and world one way or another. So, if we understand what's within us and use it as a tool for evolution and growth, then we can utilize our knowledge and intuitive input about auras for our benefit.

Understanding your own aura and your own being can help you refine your frequency. Your aura is like a brilliant musical instrument resonating outward. If you tune your cells to the frequencies that you desire to experience externally, you will resonate those frequencies out through your being and aura. You will be creating waves and fields using your thoughts and creating thought waves. This will be accomplished through the movement of photons and other elementary particles in your brain. These elements of movement and particle action, as well as the waves and fields, create resonances extending out from your brain and filling your aura and then go out into your life. So, you can harness these abilities to create your reality. We're going to go deep into that concept, and I'm going to give you numerous techniques in later chapters, so stand by for that.

As you develop that awareness of your own aura, another benefit will be observing and noticing how your aura and its frequency affects those around you. And vice versa. For example, in the chart above, we talked about the strong leadership ability and charisma of a water element person from the Taoist perspective. You can think about how that charismatic individual walks into a room, and people behave a certain way. They're inclined to favor what that water element person communicates that they want them to favor. This is not always directly stated as a verbal cue, although it could be. It is the energy and essence, the magnetism that is inherent in that individual. It makes other people want to please them and follow them, showing how one person's aura can affect the behavior of others and then affect the aura of others. You may not desire to have that effect on others. If you do, hopefully you'll wield it with integrity.

You could also apply that concept to service and altruism by holding the frequency of love and high vibration within your aura. In doing so, as long as you are fortified energetically, nutritionally, and emotionally, all the things in your strong frequency and your bright light can radiate and influence those around you.

When I first graduated college, I worked as a kindergarten teacher, and it was very apparent to me that in that setting it was easy to do because the auras of the children were primarily supporting the same intention. They were full of love, hugs, happiness, laughter, and playfulness. It allowed me to set that intention to be in the frequency of love and high vibration and hold it easily because most of the kids were holding it already. That inherent and primarily unconscious energetic support from other people and other auras let me hold that frequency more strongly in other parts of my life and influenced those in the school and the classroom who might be having a bad day and would benefit from being around the frequency of love and high vibration.

If you might identify as empathic or sensitive, that's another case of how valuable it is to know yourself. If we tend in that direction, then we know that we need to work on owning our space. We have meditations and activities for that later in the book, so keep your eyes peeled for those. When we're able to fully inhabit the totality of our auric space, we can intentionally fill our auras and have that positive effect on our environment. We also understand that our ability to be influenced needs to be modulated so we can hold the frequencies we desire in our auras to create the life we desire.

If we know that we tend to be high energy, have a lot of fiery tendencies, and have densely packed particles, then we can choose to be aware of that and work on the things that bring lightness to the mind and spaciousness to the particles. Things like deep breathing, sea salt baths, time in nature, meditation, quieting the mind, overall mindfulness, and tuning in to the subtle side of life can be helpful.

We can consider taking our fiery essence that has an abundance of energy and spreading it out further, letting our aura be a little bit bigger when it's appropriate so it won't impinge on others and so we don't feel so densely and tightly packed within ourselves. When we do that, the lowering tension within our being can spread out into our immediate family and those around us. By the way, fiery types need to be aware that sometimes their wonderfully strong energy can provoke people and/or overstimulate some. So if we were extending that aura out bigger because we have the energy to do it and it might feel good, we need to be aware of who's around us. A great time to do that is out in nature because then we can feel the interconnection of the plants, animals, and the land. They are easily able to hold that extra frequency and not be overly impacted.

When we first increase our understanding of ourselves, we can then expand our sphere out to those around us through observing and understanding their auras as well. Then we can begin to play with the exchange of energy and interconnection between us and other people. As we know, we are always aiming for complete consent and total integrity. We never want to do any harm. We want to help all and harm none in all that we do. That is one of the responsibilities of opening your intuitive and psychic abilities. It is a gift, a skill. If you misuse it, it can create collateral damage. Plus, it'll likely bounce back to you one way or another. Why would you want to be out of integrity when you can win, flourish, grow, and evolve in integrity and live the life of your dreams?

You can use the tools and resources that include your mind, heart, intuitive abilities, and all these wonderful gifts and wield them with a light hand, always in the spirit of love and helping all and harming none.

You can read the room—literally! In a meeting, at home with your kids, even with your pets, you can let yourself tune in to the auras around other people while being conscious of maintaining the structural integrity of your own aura and your space. This is how you can navigate life harmoniously and even more easily take steps forward toward whatever you desire to create.

Intuitive perceptions are a gift. Your psychic abilities that are burgeoning and growing now, and will for the rest of your life, are a bestowal. I've been a medical intuitive for 23 years, and I'm still growing in my ability, even though I've been practicing intuitive arts for almost 30 years. It's a never-ending learning process, and what a tremendous blessing it is. Why not have more information to navigate duality? Why not have more helpful data to create the life you desire?

So, steep yourself in total appreciation and gratitude for the intuitive abilities that you have and those that will be and continue to expand throughout your days. Thank yourself. Thank your world. Thank the great mystery and all that is. Because just like my late medicine teacher, Laurie, used to say, you walk in beauty.

PART IV

CLEANSING ELECTROMAGNETIC FIELDS

In this section of the book, we will step into empowerment and unleash our abilities to change our auras. We will look at how to work with auras from a shamanic perspective. I have taught beginning through expert shamanism courses for the past 23 years and learned a lot of shamanic knowledge from my late medicine teacher, Laurie. Shamanism is the process of journeying into what we call alternate reality to bring back healing and information. This practice was used for healing and gathering knowledge in almost all ancient cultures. Some classic elements of shamanism you may have heard of include power animals, animal totems, journeying with plant spirits, soul retrieval, elements of what is sometimes referred to as psychic surgery (a form of what we call shamanic extraction), and much more. The reason I have devoted part of my work to teaching shamanism is because I present it as a standardized, repeatable practice through which you can talk to your spirit guides. It puts the power in your hands! These guides can be angels, star beings, ancestors, and more. There are many ritualistic and ceremonial elements to shamanic work that are used for the maintenance of energy and our auras. These involve smoke cleansing and other ways we extract dense energy from the body and aura. Then we use shamanic techniques to refill the space with high-vibrational light.

We will also look at the medical intuitive implications of optimizing your aura for better health. You will learn how to fix cloudy auras and clear the energy of your aura. We will draw techniques and traditions from around the world and delve deeply into the energy work side of auras. When the energy of our body is healthy and the energy of our aura/biofield is healthy, we experience an optimum life. We are going to troubleshoot auras that need healing and unfold our awareness of how to accomplish this. Get ready to raise your vibration, clarify your energy, and feel great all the time. That's our intention: to feel great all the time holistically. And, that's exactly what we're going to do.

SHAMANIC AURA WORK

I was trained in an oral shamanic healing tradition by my medicine teacher, Laurie. There were a lot of intricate components to this training. Some training elements were very specific, and some elements of shamanism are relatively universal and cross-cultural. Two of them are known as extraction and retrieval. Extraction simply means the removal of something that is not for the highest good. It can apply to lots of different things, like the energy of land or homes as well as the aura and the body. Sometimes extractions are symbolic, and sometimes they show up as actual dense energy.

When working on optimizing the energy of our auras, our objective is to raise our overall vibration. Because our auras are a composite frequency of all the movement of photons in our body, when we optimize the aura, we also optimize the body. And, similarly, when we optimize the energy movement and frequency of the body, we increase the frequency of the aura.

When we utilize extraction in the aura, we are able to identify and disintegrate or remove areas of lower frequency. These can be caused by many different things, from ancestral and karmic energy to life experiences to interactions with other people and much more.

Later in this section, we will go step-by-step through some extraction techniques, and I will walk you through how to clean and clear the aura using various techniques, some of which are shamanic in nature, whether they originated that way or not.

Another universal type of endeavor in shamanic work is called a retrieval. Retrieval can apply to all kinds of things. It means retrieving power animals, spirit guide connections, soul retrieval, and much more. It means bringing something back into the aura or body that was either lost or that would be of benefit. It is adding energy to the aura, body, life, whereas extraction is subtracting.

When we do shamanic retrieval work in relation to the aura, it means that we are typically adding high-vibrational frequencies and energies to the aura to optimize and enhance it. Sometimes, when we're doing this amid a shamanic journey, things will show up symbolically, and that's how we get the information about the energy that we are adding. We will be doing shamanic retrieval energy work on our auras in the Manifesting with Aura Alchemy section.

MEDICAL INTUITIVE
AURA HEALING

When we look at the aura from medical intuitive per-spective, we look at it in conjunction with the connection to the body. Because the aura is a composite field the body generates and is formed from the myriad frequencies of all the electrically conductive components of the physical body, it has a lot of diverse energy within it. When we tune in to the aura on a larger scale, we feel the combina-tion of all that energy.

In my work as a medical intuitive, sometimes I describe myself as an archaeologist. It's like I am looking at and unearthing an ancient tablet that was buried deep, and then I'm using a little brush to remove the particulates out of the writing on it so I can read what's written there to learn what is happening in the body. I used to say that my medicine teacher, Laurie, was more like a bulldozer. She could do the archaeology work, but her specialty was bulldozing big karmic densities.

We apply both metaphors—the archaeologist and the bulldozer—in our medical intuitive aura healing work. Sometimes, we need to bulldoze out giant karmic or ancestral densities from the aura. That's when we use a lot of extraction techniques. You'll learn about many of those in the subsequent chapters on clearing.

Other times, we need to get more granular and find the specific areas of density and discern their flavor to understand what we need to do to heal. Sometimes we need to simply extract and remove them, and sometimes we need to symbolically read that complicated tablet to understand why the densities are present in the aura. It could be because an ancestor experienced an auric trauma, and that frequency was passed down through the energetic DNA in the body.

It could also be because the person experienced trauma, and it affected their aura. One example of that is people who have been assaulted, where the boundary of their aura has not been respected by others. Sometimes these people have a challenge maintaining a balanced boundary of their personal space. It's completely understandable that that would be the case. In that situation, we can fortify the aura and help the person who has experienced another person disregarding their boundaries feel safer.

That aura is our personal bubble and represents our security and our feeling of safety. If we don't feel safe in the world for any reason, sometimes that can show up in our aura. An example of that is not only someone who has directly experienced trauma but also someone whose parents or grandparents have.

I can recall a client who was exposed to what ended up being frightening information in grade school. This exposure was completely well-meaning by the parents wanting to educate the child about types of assaults and how to protect oneself. Perhaps it was delivered a little bit too early. If the child was a highly sensitive person (HSP), that information may have made the child feel unsafe and gotten stuck in their brain and energy. As an adult, that person might feel like they need to scrub their brain to get that imprint out. There's absolutely no judgment on those parents because they were legitimately trying to protect their child and had likely witnessed or experienced some traumatic events that motivated them to start that process of trying to create safety too early.

This is a case where the frequency of the parents and the information to which the child was exposed affected the adult. So that adult had to work on fortifying their aura, owning their space, and feeling safe. Sometimes that adult would feel triggered in situations that were not dangerous but echoed something that they heard, like a story from their parents about where the situation ended up being dangerous. In those cases, that adult had the challenge of working on filling the aura with the essence of feeling good all the time while also noticing and releasing attachment to feelings of fear that would come up and be triggered.

In some of the activities contained in this section of the book, you'll learn how to do general clearings and releases that can usually help overcome these kinds of imprints. In the Alchemy section of the book, you will learn how to refill and replace the space in the aura that you've cleared out with specific high-frequency energies. We always do a little bit of that at the end of our clearing exercises. Whenever you extract, if there is an open space left, then you want to fill it with high-vibrational energy.

In my medical intuitive work, I always say that the highest vibration in the known universe is joy. Whenever you clear a space in the aura or the body, you want to refill it with high-frequency bright white light that is at the frequency of joy or similar. You can use the number

3,333,333 or higher if you'd like. Some people like to use 8,888,888 as an abundance frequency. Ask for the highest vibrational energy to refill any space that you clear out. I will remind you of this in the clearing chapter so you can make sure to use that technique.

The crux of the medical intuitive side of auric work is the same as how I approach my intuitive work in the body: raising the frequency of the areas in question and the whole composite of the body and biofield.

The higher we raise our vibration, the better we feel and the more high-frequency energy we funnel into this dimension through our existence. Sometimes when people are seeking their life's purpose or dharma, the thing that I bring them back to is the higher your frequency is, then the higher the vibrational light you channel into this planet through your existence. By doing so, you raise your vibration and the vibration of the planet. The higher we raise the frequency of the planet, the better life will be on Earth. All the things that cause suffering in our reality for all life and all sentient beings on Earth are lower-vibrational frequency. By raising the frequency of ourselves and our planet, eventually we can achieve an end to suffering on the planet. Contributing to that is part of my life's mission, and it's part of all our missions, one way or another.

In my medical intuitive work, at times I end up viewing things at a quantum level and finding how we need to, for example, optimize the frequency of a gene in the body and change the DNA in the body to create less suffering. When we create less suffering, we raise the frequency of the person, and we're continuing our journey of healing ourselves and the planet.

You'll notice that in this book, I sometimes use the words *vibration* and *frequency* interchangeably. Both words in this case simply mean if we were to assign a numerical value to energy and electricity and/or assign an emotional or descriptive value to it, you can see how the emotion of *joy* describes the highest frequency, vibration, and energy. You could use *love* for that as well, especially if you're referring to unconditional, universal love. Another great word to utilize is *bliss*, which combines the ideas of joy and happiness with a sense of contentment and comfort. There are all kinds of ways to describe vibrational energies and energetic frequencies. It can be a great idea to get familiar with some of the descriptive words that indicate the highest-frequency energies so you can use them in your daily life. It can be through speaking them or using them in an affirmative context internally to create states of high-frequency energy in your body and your aura.

Read on to learn the techniques to clear density from your aura and thereby raise its frequency. Then, when you enter the Alchemy section, we will harness the incredible power of elementary particles and their waves and infinite fields to create the lives we desire that contain continual high-frequency energy that leaves us feeling great all the time.

ANCESTRAL AURIC IMPRINTS

Our auras can hold imprints of our ancestors' auras, lives, and bodies. We talked about a few examples of that in previous chapters, including how the encodements and energetic information contained in the egg of the egg that made us is imprinted to varying degrees on the inside layer of the outer shell of our aura.

We've also talked about how fears that our ancestors possessed can be translated into our auras and impact our sense of safety. Our auras can be imprinted with the energy of our ancestors in many ways. If an ancestor suffered a physical injury in a certain area, and the energy of the trauma, pain, and discomfort got stuck in the ancestor's body or aura, sometimes that can be passed down through the generations. It does not mean that every single descendant will exhibit it. It means that certain descendants may. One way to think of it is that those souls choose to embody that ancestral density to eventually clear it out of the family line. That is an example of evolution and action.

As far as I have able to tell after 23 years as a medical intuitive, one of the reasons souls choose to incarnate in human bodies is to further human evolution. Albeit that happens sometimes slowly over numerous generations that process out density from a family line. I often tell my medical clients when we're uncovering something like this that if it was up to me, it would not be orchestrated in this way. I am just the messenger. I don't fully understand why human suffering exists. And why I, as a soul, chose to tacitly endorse this system of duality by incarnating in it.

When things are at an ancestral level in the body, meaning they're not directly a result of something the person currently living experienced, we often see echoes in the aura. These things are obviously also present with certain physical ailments and genetic situations, but we have a unique tendency to hold ancestral density as well as positive ancestral energy in the aura. This is because it is a field devoid of the constraints of matter. It's pure energy and unencumbered by fermions, which are the building blocks of matter. As you know, our aura intersects with matter in the air and the gases around us as well as with the neutrinos coursing through it. But the actual aura is made of bosons, which are force and charge carriers. That makes those particles uniquely suited to carry imprints of energy.

When we undertake different kinds of aura cleansing, we have an opportunity to clear those ancestral patterns that no longer serve us. One of the benefits of regularly cleansing your own aura is removing more of those low-vibration ancestral layers. Sometimes densities and low-vibrational energies make their way into the body if they are present in the aura for a long time. We can practice great energetic hygiene and clean our aura using the wide variety of techniques listed in this chapter to prevent health imbalances as well as clear ourselves of limiting beliefs that our ancestors may have held. This also helps us clear out tendencies that are counterproductive to our intentions and way of life. That means ways that we might react without thinking to situations in our lives that are not from us but a result of tendencies from our ancestral line and those imprints and echoes are resonating through our aura and body. So, let's clear those all out and make space for high-vibrational energy and the experience of feeling good all the time and living a life of joy.

CLEARING
YOUR AURA

Let's dive into the mechanics of cleaning and clearing the aura. We will be removing lower-vibrational energy using a variety of techniques and replacing it with high-vibrational energy. With all techniques, we will always follow the clearing with an infusion of high-vibrational white light and joy so we always fill the space that we clear with higher-frequency energy. That's an important component of owning your space in terms of your aura. You need to fill your aura with your essence to fortify it and keep the frequency high. That's also how we maintain good boundaries, not only energetically but also emotionally and mentally.

It is especially important for empaths and highly sensitive people to be extra conscious of owning their space and filling it with their own individual essence so they are not impacted by other people easily. It's a good rule for everybody and helps us maintain good health and a happy life because our frequency is high.

JOURNEYING INTO YOUR AURA

As we move into medical intuitive techniques to clear the aura, we will first begin with a process to journey into your aura. The idea of journeying originates in shamanic work. When we journey in a shamanic manner, we travel to what is known as alternate reality to bring back healing and information. In those cases, we either perform extraction or retrieval, or we do something called psychopomp work, which involves spirits that have crossed to the other side.

We will do a guided meditation now to help you journey into your own aura. When you journey into alternate reality, one of the places that you can go to is the middle world. That is the here and now on this earthly plane of existence. We will be doing a middle world journey and looking at the energy of your aura.

This process will echo cross-cultural shamanic techniques, but I have adapted it to a beginner level because most of you will not have taken shamanic classes. Typically, when we undertake a shamanic journey, we use something to shift our brain waves. When I teach shamanism, I use the beat of the drum, and I play that live. Other types of shamanic work use a variety of techniques to shift your brain waves. In our case today, we're going to use some deep breathing and relaxation to do so. If you would like, you can go to AmyLeighMercreeree.com /auraalchemyresourcces and use the audio I created for you to enhance your experience. This audio has live drumming to help shift your brain waves. If you don't use that right now, it's okay. The process can work through reading this text as well.

Guided Aura Journey Process

Begin by taking some deep breaths into your lower abdomen and imagine that you're filling your torso from bottom to top, as if it was a paper bag. Make your inhalations long and slow as you fill your torso with air, and when you exhale after holding for a few seconds, stretch the exhalation out and blow through pursed lips as if you're blowing through a straw. Cycle this breathing and create longer and longer stretches of exhalation for a few minutes. Get yourself nicely relaxed and oxygenated.

Next, repeat the following aloud or in your mind to set intention for your process: "I ask that all that transpires in this journey into my aura be for the very highest good of all life and in accordance with universal natural law, helping all and harming none. I ask that whatever is for my highest and best interest will come through easily and gently and that I be protected fully during this process. I welcome the presence of my highest vibrational guides, guards, and teams and thank them for their help. I set an intention to journey into my aura to bring back healing and information for my highest good."

Begin your journey process. See yourself in front of a gate. It may look like a doorway or an archway. Feel your spirit guides all around. You can work with whatever spirit guide resonates for you at this time. Some suggestions are Archangel Raphael, the goddess Brigit, the Hindu deity Ganesha, or one of your highest vibrational ancestors. Feel one or all these beings. They are with you at the gate or doorway. In a moment, you will go together through this opening, and you will be entering your own aura from the outside looking in. When you enter this realm, do so with a totally open mind and be receptive to all types of input: thoughts, feelings, sights, sounds, smells, words, colors, textures, emotions, and ideas. It will be like you're walking into another realm, and you'll be miniature, so you will have lots of space inside your aura.

When you're ready after you've taken some deep breaths, gotten centered, and felt your spirit family around you, with your eyes closed, allow yourself walk forward and open the gate, archway, or door and go through. Once you are within, look around, feel around, sense around. You can fly in this journey, so fly around through the space of the aura and notice the sensations and information that comes to you. Be totally open and receptive.

After you've floated around without an agenda and taken in the sights, sounds, and smells, you can move up to the top and check out the area above the head and then from there go down around the body and check out all the different areas of the aura, noticing differences and sensing flavors and sensations. Do this with no judgment, just complete acceptance. You can note any areas that feel like they need specific clearing. You can also notice the areas that feel really good and where the frequency is high. This is just an exploratory journey.

Continue this process for as long as you'd like. Gather all the information and experience you desire; then when you're ready, exit through the doorway or gate in which you entered with your guide(s). Then see yourself outside it again as if you're looking at it. Feel yourself present in your body and open your eyes. State aloud, "I am here now," over and over to bring yourself back to your body. Pat your arms and legs and make sure you feel fully present to yourself before returning your day. Ground yourself by focusing on your five senses.

Guided Practice to Fix Cloudy Auras

When you have noticed a sensation of your aura being cloudy, whether it's your journey into your aura or just in general, there is a specific fix. Along with all the clearing techniques detailed below, you can use this practice to bring clear energy and remove confusion from the aura. To do this we will work with the Hindu deity Ganesha. Ganesha is incredibly helpful in clearing away obstacles and bringing clarity to our lives.

Take a few deep breaths and get yourself centered. Say this: "I ask that all that transpires in the entirety of this aura process be for the very highest good of all life, helping all and harming none. I asked that whatever is for my highest good come through and occur easily and gently and that I be protected fully during this process. I welcome the presence of my highest vibrational guides, guards, and teams and thank them for their help. I set an intention to partner with Ganesha to bring clarity to my aura and remove any cloudiness. It is done."

Invite Ganesha to sit across from you. You can just say the word *yes* to Ganesha, who's already in the room with you. Feel him right in front of your aura so the front of your body is facing him and the space between the two of you is filled with your aura and his aura. Notice with your spirit eyes how Ganesha, although he's in a nonphysical form, still has an aura around him. He, too, has a composite energy field of his being that extends out around him.

Feel like you're looking Ganesha in the eyes as you're sitting facing one another. As your eyes meet Ganesha's spirit eyes, feel a sense of connection with him. Feel his neutral love for you and his healing capabilities. Tell him that he has permission now to remove any cloudiness from your aura and bring about clarity on all levels. You can say that out loud or in your mind to him.

Next, place your hands out in front of you with your palms facing outward. Feel Ganesha reach through the space of your aura and place his spirit hands palm-to-palm with yours. As this connection is made, feel reverberations and waves of energy coming out of the intersection of the two of your hands. It may look like concentric circles moving out through you and your aura. It is the frequency of clarity and is a high-frequency energy. You may repeat the word *yes* like a mantra to receive the healing from Ganesha and allow waves of clarity to move out and through you. They will remove obstacles, density, and any cloudiness from your aura and bring total clarity to you for all time. Say yes to Ganesha and accept this healing.

When that is completed, it will feel like the transmission of energy between you and Ganesha is subsiding. When that occurs, you can bring your hands down and tell him thank you. If you feel inclined, you can invite him to give you an energetic hug. If so, feel like he moves forward, and as the two of your auras get closer and closer and interconnected, wrap your arms gently around one another, engaging in a benevolent hug. You can tell him thank you again and feel your heart connected to his heart in an eternal, unconditional loving communion.

ENERGY CLEARING
TECHNIQUES

Below, you'll find instructions for different kinds of energy clearing techniques to be used for your aura. Most would fall under the umbrella of shamanic extraction, insofar as they are subtracting density from the aura. They also have a component of retrieval because we will refill the spaces cleared with high-vibrational energy. Each one will lead you through the process step-by-step and prompt you to refill your aura with high-vibrational light. Enjoy the process of enacting each of these and thank your higher self for bringing you this book to help you gain clarity and experience a high-frequency life through these techniques.

SHAMANIC EXTRACTION AURA CLEARING TECHNIQUE

Center yourself with some deep breathing. State aloud or in your mind: "I ask that all that transpires in the entirety of this clearing technique session be for the very highest good of all life. And, in accordance with universal natural law, helping all and harming none. This entire endeavor is for my highest and best interest. I welcome the presence of my highest vibrational guides and thank them for their help."

With your eyes closed, feel yourself connect with your spirit family. Call the Hindu deity known as Kali Ma. Do this by saying the following: "I invite Kali Ma to enter my space at this time. I invite you here with love and care and request that you perform shamanic extraction on my aura for my highest good. I am so grateful for your help."

Kail-Ma, also known as Kali, is a goddess from Hindu traditions known to be a master of transmutation. She is very helpful in taking dense energy and basically eating it to transform it into pure white light. Feel Kali's presence in your space now. Know that she is going to guide you and help you in this process.

Close your eyes and invite Kali to place her palms over your eyes very gently. This will be with her spirit hands. She will use her spirit hands to help you see with what is often called the second sight. She may also place her palms over your forehead so you can see intuitively as well and picture things in your mind. With your eyes closed and the assistance of Kali, allow yourself to tune in to the space all around you in a bubble for three feet in all directions.

Without thinking, simply allow your awareness to travel to the first place that requires shamanic extraction. You are now there. Snap your fingers three times in this area. If you can't exactly reach, just do the best you can with that geographically in the aura. As you snap your fingers three times, say, "All is well. All is well."

When you snap your fingers, it will extract the density from the aura. Kali is helping. Then, move to the next place. Go to the second spot without thinking. Snap your fingers three times and repeat the process.

Do this at least three more times to do a minimum of five extractions in the aura, and you can do more. When this completes, thank Kali for her help and envision a cascade of pure white light, like a giant golden faucet up above you has been turned on. It and the light are made of pure joy. Let this pure white light cascade down through the top of your aura and down through your body and your whole aura from top to bottom like a powerful waterfall of joy. Receive it saying the word *yes* and the word *joy*. Repeat the word *joy* over and over. Say this: "I am filled with joy from top to bottom in all directions. My frequency is high, and I am pure joy. Thank you, Kali Ma. It is done."

Return your presence to the space and make sure you feel absolutely rooted within yourself before continuing with your day.

SMOKE CLEANSING AND SOUND CLEANSING

Clearing your aura using either the smoke of flammable botanicals or sound waves have some things in common. Using burning dried herbs imparts the botanical essence of these plants into your aura while also using the medium of their smoke to act as a physical substance to clean the energy and space around your body. You can also use this for the body, so in the description of how to enact these cleanses, we will do the aura and the body so you can get a thorough clearing. It makes sense for us to clear the energy of the body and the aura because, as you know, the aura is a composite field generated by the photons moving through the body.

Clearing with sound waves that you generate specifically for that purpose has a similar effect. The sound waves move through your aura and body, dislodging density and stuck energy. In both cases, when we apply intention, we magnify the process.

The practical application has to do with moving the medium, whether it is sound or smoke spatially through all areas of the aura and around all areas of the body, including above the head and below the feet. We do this to make sure we clear everything geographically in the auric egg.

In this chapter, you'll find two tables. The first will talk to you about the properties of potential dried herbs that you can utilize for smoke cleansing. And underneath that, you will find another table that provides you with some ideas for different types of ways to generate sound waves for clearing purposes and some of the specific applications for that.

These are starting points, but any smoke-generating botanical and any sound-generating instrument will do the job. No need to be picky about what you use, but it can be fun to look at all the possibilities.

Herbal Cleansing

Flammable Botanical	Properties	Spirit Guides to Invoke
Dried mint flowers, leaves, and stems	Refreshing, cleansing	Hindu goddess Lakshmi
Dried mugwort leaves	Opens intuition, promotes lucid dreaming	Welsh goddess Rhiannon
Dried sage leaves and stems	Grounding, drying, cleansing	American Indian grandmother White Buffalo Woman
Dried rosemary flowers, leaves, and stems	Promotes clarity, stimulating	Roman goddess Hygea
Dried thyme flowers, leaves, and stems	Promotes enjoyment of music and poetry, creative	Hindu goddess Saraswati
Dried oregano leaves and stems	Antimicrobial, antifungal, antibacterial, invigorating	Greek mythological deity Hermes

Flammable Botanical	Properties	Spirit Guides to Invoke
Dried lavender flowers, leaves, and stems	Raises frequency, opens heart and mind, clears pericardium channel (TCM)	Roman goddess Flora
Dried juniper leaves	Activating, raises spirits, encouraging	Norse mythological deity Thor
Dried rose petals	Heart opening, allows us to feel love, promoting yin and feminine essence	Greek goddess Aphrodite
Palo santo wood	Activates mystical energies, invokes precision and clarity	Aztec mythological deity Quetzalcoatl
Dried basil flowers, leaves, and stems	Freshens the mind, catalyzes the heart	Celtic goddess Ceridwyn
Dried marjoram leaves	Provides inspiration and insight	Yakut goddess Aisyt
Dried dill leaves	Invokes abundance and a sense of nourishment	Roman goddess Abundantia
Dried lemongrass leaves and stalks	Helps us embrace the unfamiliar and begin a new cycle	Thai/Buddhist goddess Nang Kwak
Dried lemon balm flowers	Promotes emotional balance, vitality	Mesopotamian goddess Astarte
Dried mullein leaves	Dries internal dampness and relieve nasal congestion (TCM), connects higher consciousness	Berber (North African) goddess Neith
Dried damiana leaves	Invokes pleasure and joy	Yoruba goddess Yemayá
Dried marshmallow root and leaves	Promotes yin especially in kidney channels, increases discernment	Asian goddess Chang'é
Dried dandelion flowers, leaves, stems, and roots	Creates movement in liver and gallbladder channels (TCM), promotes creativity and exuberance	Irish goddess Danu
Dried raspberry leaves	Tonifies kidney channels and promotes reproductive health, progesterone promoting, fosters femininity and unconditional acceptance of self	Sumerian goddess Inanna

Instructions to Prepare Your Flammable Botanicals

You can purchase your herbs predried. Or, you can dry on your own by hanging the stems with leaves and any flowers still attached upside down, tied with a cotton string. Leave for a week or so and check the progress.

To smoke cleanse, you can use a few different methods. You can prepare the botanicals and place them in a heat-safe vessel. Some people use an abalone shell, or you can use a stainless-steel bowl placed on a trivet or silicon mat made for high heat. You can experiment with different heat-safe vessels. You're going to want to be able to hold it easily and have your hand protected from the heat. And you want to be able to move it around through the area around your body so you can cleanse all different parts of your aura. Have oven mitts handy. Use a long match or grill lighter to light the botanicals.

Depending on the type of materials you have available, if you're able to obtain the stalk or stem with the leaves and/or flowers attached, then you can use cotton string to tie those in a bundle to use for your smoke cleansing. You can tie them together on a piece of palo santo wood to hold them firm if you'd like. In all the smoke cleansing methods, you can combine any of the ingredients listed above. You can also use other types of plants, but make sure to do a thorough check to be sure that they are not poisonous when burned or touched.

Carefully monitor the botanicals continually while they are burning. Warn children of the risk of fire, and store all matches and lighters up high. Light the botanical so it emits a stream of smoke. You will be "sprinkling" the smoke throughout your aura. You will use your intention to focus on each area of your aura, often starting from top to bottom and perhaps moving left to right, front to back, to make sure you cover every square inch of space.

You can also think about your intention and envision the smoke moving through the physical body and clearing that too. Be thorough and make sure to bring your attention and intention to every little nook of your aura and body to get a thorough cleansing.

Please be extra careful to avoid flammable surfaces and fabrics like curtains. Ideally, smoke cleansing is done outside in a nonflammable environment. Make sure you check for dry conditions if your area is prone to wildfires. If it's windy, that's another time to avoid outdoor smoke cleansing. Alternatively, you can also do this next to an open window. Be conscious of the placement of smoke detectors.

Sound Cleansing

Instrument or Sound Type	Properties	Spirit Guides to Invoke
Chime	Clearing, lyrical	Buddhist goddess Quan Yin
Ting Cha (yoga cymbals)	Easy to maneuver, cleansing	Hindu mythological deity Shiva
Drum	Powerful, empowering	African goddess Oya
Rattle	Specific, clears small subtle energies	Incan goddess Pachamama
Singing bowl (all types)	All-encompassing, resonant	Buddhist mythological figure Guatama Buddha
Didgeridoo (D note recommended for clearing aura and body)	Strong, sturdy, potent	Australian aboriginal goddess Yhi
Recorded sounds or music	Varies according to content	Greek mythological deity Apollo

General Smoke and Sound Cleansing Procedure

Prepare your botanicals or hold your instrument or sound-producing device. State your intention clearly saying something like, "I ask that all that transpires in the entirety of this cleansing process for the very highest good of all life and in accordance with the universal natural law, helping all and harming none. I ask that my aura and body are completely cleared of all density and any vibratory frequencies that are lower than 3,333,333. I ask that I am filled with high-vibrational light and joy and anything that is not of the light is easily and completely removed from my aura, body, home, car, and life for all time. It is done."

You can add whatever else you would like and then move the smoking botanicals or the sound instrument through your aura. Start at either the top or the bottom, wherever you feel guided. See that point at least three feet above your head or below your feet. Then begin to move down or up, getting each corner, each edge, and each space in between. Imagine that you're looking at your aura and your body like three-dimensional graph paper. You need to make sure the smoke or the sound goes through every single square. Use your intention, which is your attention, in each little space, making sure that you completely saturate your whole aura and your whole body with this cleansing smoke or sound. Take your time and be extra-thorough.

It can be valuable to go through the whole auric bubble multiple times and make sure that you have a comprehensive cleanse. Once that is complete, you can extinguish any flammable material or put down your instrument or sound device and then visualize a giant faucet high above you that is made of gold. It's much bigger than you. Turn the faucet on. Notice it's very easy to turn. See bright white light cascading out of this faucet in a continual steady stream. This bright white light is the highest vibrational energy. It's made of pure light, pure joy, and pure love.

Watch it cascade down through your aura and your body, filling every space that has been vacated by denser frequencies. Watch it fill every single inch of your body and your aura. Say, yes, and you can use the word, *joy* like a mantra. Feel the power of joy pulsing through your arms, hands, legs, feet, torso, head, neck, and your whole aura as you radiate pure joy. It's pouring down and rushing through you—ever renewing, ever rejuvenating—filling you with the highest-frequency energy possible. Say, yes to it and receive this bestowal of pure light from the Divine.

You can leave the faucet running, understanding that it will follow you around all the time. You can always update and renew it and bring your attention to it again whenever you desire. Make sure you thank all your spirit family and your higher self and any spirit guides that you feel were helpful in the process.

If there is any botanical material left in your vessel, you can discard that, ideally outside on the ground once it's completely extinguished. You can keep the unburned plant material for next time.

SALT CLEANSING

Set an intention before your salt clearing about what you'd like to accomplish. You can adapt one from our other cleansing methods or create a new one. Make sure you ask that all that transpires in the entirety of your cleansing session be for the very highest good of all life.

Salt clearing can be done in lots of different ways, and there's no wrong way to do it. For salt cleansing of the aura, it is best to use untreated salt. This can include salts that are labeled things like Celtic, Hawaiian, or Himalayan.

You can enact your salt cleansing anywhere you'd like. I would recommend either doing it outdoors or in the shower to minimize the mess. If you do it outdoors, be aware that salt can affect plants, so you might decide to do it on dirt or an area of the yard where you're not concerned about having a lot of vegetation. You could also do it on your driveway or pavement, as needed. Of course, it's always best to put our bare feet in some real dirt or vegetation, but a patio or pavement will also suffice.

So, whether you are performing your salt cleansing in the shower or outdoors, you can use a large quantity of salt, and if you have a big untreated sea salt container that you dedicated the cleansing to, you just use it straight out of there. You'll mostly hold the dispenser up high above you and use the power of gravity to make the salt cascade down from its container. Sprinkle it liberally through your aura, reaching as high you can all around you. Pour it straight onto the crown of your head, clearing your crown chakra too. This part can help with headaches. Use the salt to clear your aura, getting it through every part of your aura, kind of like we did with our smoke cleansing.

If you want to do an extensive salt clearing and you're in the shower and can rinse it off right away, pour lots of salt right onto the crown of your head. Plus pour even more, all over your scalp, and with your eyes and mouth closed, all over your face. Next, saturate the throat and whole body and use it as a dry salt scrub, especially making sure you scrub under your arms. You can clean and clear your energy on every level. If you're doing this in the shower, it goes right down the drain and dissolves, releasing it back into the earth. If you're doing it outside, it just goes on the surface of the earth and dissolves next time there is rain or moisture. It's the perfect way to release dense energy.

A little medical intuitive pro tip: when we apply salt to the outside of the physical body, from a traditional Chinese medicine perspective we are bringing what is called the *wei chi* to the surface. That is the external chi. It protects us from not only energetic invaders but also from pathogens. So, if you've been exposed to cold or flu and want to bring your immunity and your external chi to the surface to hold it at bay, you can do a salt clearing and salt scrub to accomplish that. I remind all my medical intuitive clients every time I talk to them that I am not a doctor. All health information is just that: information. You are always directed to consult your health practitioner about anything medical and any information I provide you. It is all supplemental, nonclinical, and informative only.

EGG CLEANSING

Multiple cultures use the process of egg cleansing to remove density from the body, and we will also use it for the aura. You will use an actual uncooked egg. State your intention for the cleansing process, making sure to say that everything that transpires during it be for the very highest good of all life.

Move the egg over what you perceive as the inside layer of your aura. Move it through each corner of your aura, just like we did in our other cleansings. Then roll it over the surface of your body. Let all the dense energy or anything that it's time for you to release go into the egg.

When that feels complete, take it outdoors if possible into a wooded area and crack the egg onto the ground and look at what you see. Allow yourself to receive any visionary or psychic input from that. Leave the shells on the earth as well.

If you don't have access to an appropriate outdoor space, you can crack it into a disposable cup that is ideally clear. Look at the inside the egg and allow yourself to receive any intuitive input. Then, you can either flush the liquid down the toilet or pour it outside and place the shells and the cup in the garbage, ideally taking that garbage out of the house immediately after.

WATER CLEANSING METHODS

When you begin any of the water cleansing processes, always state your intention clearly, asking that all that transpires be for the very highest good of all life. Most of us are fortunate enough to have one of the best water cleansing methods available in our bathrooms: the shower! A shower is an absolutely fabulous way to use water to cleanse our auras and to release what has come out of the aura down the drain. You can use the spray from the shower and move it through every area of your aura the best that you can, releasing what no longer serves you down the drain. Pretty simple. We kind of do some form of that every time we take a shower. If you'd like to open and create warmth of heart and mind, you can use warmer or hot water. If you'd like to clear, invigorate, and refresh, you can use colder water.

Baths can have a cleansing effect; the difference is you are able to release a little more deeply and allow all that doesn't serve you to be set free when you send the water down the drain. You can also utilize various materials like salts, essential oils, and other compounds to create a bath experience that has a certain energy to help you let go of things and then refill you with botanical and mineral goodness.

DIY Aromatherapy Aura Cleansing Mists

Another way to clear your aura is by creating an aura cleansing mist. You can make this yourself using a wide variety of ingredients. Below, I've included a list of many possible ingredients and their properties. You can choose any, or all, of them. Simply place the ingredients in a spray bottle filled with spring or distilled water—bonus points if it is made of glass as opposed to plastic. Then, use the spray bottle and spray liberally through your entire aura, misting away any density and refilling the space with these beautiful ingredients.

Make lots of aromatherapy mist, if you desire, in a bunch of bottles. I would recommend choosing an essence or feeling that you want to feel and then placing the ingredients in the bottle with that intention. Perhaps you can write that intention on the bottle. Then it would be your mist for that purpose. That means you would be cleansing your aura with the water and ingredients and then refilling your aura with that feeling or energy. You could repeat the word like a mantra over and over as you spray it through your aura. Here are some suggestions for aura essence mantras: joy, bliss, happiness, unconditional love, peace of mind, serenity, tranquility, contentment, pleasure, ecstasy, clarity, peacefulness, wonder, adventure, effervescence, or playfulness.

Ingredient	Properties
Sea salt	Energetically cleansing
Flower essences of your choosing	Refined and subtle energies added to the aura
Trace mineral drops	Clears energy and activates aura
Epsom salt (magnesium sulfate)	Brings the essence of deep knowing of the primordial to the aura

I have created a table of essential oils and their properties for your aura sprays. The oils listed are safe for topical use and inhalation. Be sure to use therapeutic grade and ideally organic essential oils. Avoid any synthetic fragrances as they contain various undisclosed scent chemicals and ingredients used as fragrance dispersants, including diethyl phthalate. These are associated with allergies, dermatitis, respiratory distress, and reproductive system and endocrine disruption and ailments.

Add one to five drops of each oil as desired. Never spray essential oils in eyes or directly on mucous membranes unless under the care of an aromatherapist.

Essential Oil	Properties	Caution: Avoid if
Bergamot	Uplifting, happiness	In direct sun
Cardamom	Aphrodisiac, emotional warmth	None
Cedarwood	Calming, grounding	You are pregnant
Celery	Peacefulness, letting go of density and dampness (TCM)	You are pregnant
Chamomile	Patience, serenity	You are pregnant
Clary Sage	Clear mind and aura	You are pregnant

Essential Oil	Properties	Caution: Avoid if
Cypress	Comforting and simultaneously dynamic	You are pregnant
Frankincense	Spiritual connection	None
Geranium	Dancing light, happiness	You are pregnant
Ginger	Heats up the heart and libido, moves stagnant energy in small intestine meridian (TCM)	You have sensitive skin
Grapefruit	Bliss, refreshing	In direct sun
Helichriysum	Meditation, regenerating cells	None
Jasmine	Builds kidney channel yang energy (TCM), inspires sensuality and desire	You are pregnant
Lavender	Inspiration, sensing subtle energy, high vibrational	You are pregnant
Lemon	Vitality, tonifies kidney channel (TCM)	In direct sun
Lemongrass	Clears a path to high-vibrational living and realizing your heart's desires	You have sensitive skin
Lime	Moves chi in liver channel (TCM) releases sadness	In direct sun
Myrrh	Clears ancestral density	You are pregnant
Myrtle	Aids in healthy breathing, enhances mindfulness	None
Neroli	Ecstatic joy, healthy sensory pleasure	None
Orange	Centering, lowers cholesterol	In direct sun, or you have migraines
Patchouli	Connection to the earth and physical body	None
Peppermint	Invigorating	You are pregnant

Essential Oil	Properties	Caution: Avoid if
Pine	Warms kidney channel (TCM), awakens higher self	None
Rose absolute or otto	Unconditional love and acceptance for self and others	You are pregnant
Sandalwood	Meditation, roots in the earth, presence	None
Valerian	Sedative, releasing, forgiveness	You are pregnant
Vanilla	Spiritual faith, aphrodisiac	None
Vetiver	Deep connection to self and the earth	None
Ylang-ylang	Feminine energy, playfulness, open mindedness	None

CLEANSING MEDITATIONS

Sheets of Light Meditation

Get nice and comfortable and do some deep breathing to center yourself. Then state this, aloud or in your mind: "I ask that all that transpires during the entirety of this meditation be for the very highest good of all life and in accordance with universal natural law, helping all and harming none."

Next, say, "I invoke the cleansing power of pure white light. I welcome the assistance of Avalokiteshvara." This helpful bodhisattva is known by the name Avalokiteshvara. The Chinese referred to this being as Guanyin and some Buddhist scholars equate this being with the goddess Quan Yin. He/she/they is associated with pure light and compassion.

Feel the presence of your spirit helpers and together invoke a large sheet of pure, high-vibrational white light about six feet below you. This sheet stretches out around you and much farther. It's about 20 feet by 20 feet in size. See the sheet rippling as if it were in a gentle breeze.

With your intention combined with the intention of Avalokiteshvara, together raise the sheet, keeping it on a flat horizontal plane. Bring it up through the bottom of your aura. Simply watch it raise itself. You are invoking the healing process. It doesn't take any effort on your part. Observe the sheet rising up through your aura, through your body, all the way up till it stops eventually six feet above you.

Watch the sheet bundle itself up, wrapping everything that that ended up on top of it in the bundle. Observe Avalokiteshvara as they tie it off, wave to you, blow you a kiss, and fly the bundle straight into the sun, where the bundle and its contents are transmuted into white light. Watch Avalokiteshvara emerge, flying out of the sun, giving you a wave, and disappearing.

Turn on your giant golden faucet in the sky so pure white light and joy is pouring down through you and be refilled.

Say thank you to all involved.

Aura Scrubbing Meditation

Center yourself with a few minutes of deep breathing. Next, say this: "I ask that all that transpires in the entirety of this aura scrubbing meditation be for the very highest good of all life and in accordance with universal natural law, helping all and harming none. I welcome the presence of my highest vibrational guides, guards, and teams and thank them for their help. I ask that I be protected fully during this process."

Now, we will invoke the Greek and Roman goddess Hygeia to give your aura a good scrubbing and teach you the process. State aloud or internally, "Dearest Hygeia, please join me now and accept my immense gratitude for your presence. I invite you to teach me how to maintain a pristine aura and energy body for my highest good, optimum health, and to feel great all the time. I give you permission to scrub down my aura and my energy body in all ways for my highest good. Thank you so much."

Feel Hygeia before you. In a moment, lay back with your eyes closed and feel her step up to you; it will most likely be on your right side. You can tell her that you're giving her permission and allow her to begin by holding your right hand in her spirit hands. Let the connection be established. Then move into communion with her. Feel your heart and her heart pulsing energy back and forth. Then you can tell her, "I give you permission to scrub my aura and energy body." She will begin to do so. You can simply relax and receive, or if you want to observe with your spirit eyes, you can do that so you learn how to do it for yourself. There will be a unique process for your body and aura.

Observe it. It will likely appear that she is starting on the top right of your biofield and moving side to side or down in a spiral around your aura, then moving inward. She will send streams of light through your physical body and clear that energy as well. You can be aware of it all or let yourself drift off to sleep. Either way, when you wake up or when you feel the process is complete, simply thank one another and share gratitude and acknowledgment.

When the process completes, you should feel it. You will sense her back at your side, holding your right hand, then she'll let go and step back. You can talk to her like a trusted friend about whatever you want during the whole process. Make sure you thank her. Fill your entire body and aura with high-vibrational white light to fill the spaces that have been scrubbed. Sense and notice how you feel.

Then, get back up, stretch, and make sure you feel fully present to yourself. Drink plenty of water after this process. Pat your arms and legs and feel yourself present in your body.

High-Vibe Joy Auric Clearing

Do some deep breathing and make sure you feel fully centered. Then state aloud or internally, "I ask that all that transpires during this high-vibe joy cleansing be for the very highest good of all life and in accordance with universal natural law, helping all and harming none. I ask that I be protected fully during this process, and I welcome the presence of my highest vibrational guides, guards, and teams."

In this cleansing process, we will use the power of joy, which is the highest vibration in the known universe, to clear your aura. We will do this by filling your aura with the energy of joy. This energy is so powerful, it will push out and dematerialize density. In this case, we will be clearing anything dense and low-vibrational from the aura, and then we've already used the frequency of joy to refill it.

To do this, you will repeat the word *joy* like a mantra. Stay focused on it, feeling it, sensing it, and embodying its high vibration. As you repeat the word *joy*, you will feel white light coming up from beneath you and moving up through you and the whole room. It will travel up, eventually landing high above you, so the whole room, your aura, and your body are all encompassed in the energy of joy. Do this by stating the word over and over and focusing on it with relentless precision. Visualize the white light, and you can picture gold sparkles in that white light, if you choose.

Enact this process for 5 to 10 minutes or until it feels complete. Then, sense your body and the space around it. Feel how light you feel. Sense how you've cleared density and refilled the space with joy in one process. Thank yourself and your spirit guides. Make sure you feel fully present to yourself before continuing with your day.

Ancestral Auric Cleaning

For this cleansing process, you will work with the spirits of your ancestors. After doing some deep breathing and centering yourself, repeat the following words aloud or in your mind: "I ask that all that transpires during this cleansing session be for the very highest good of all life and in accordance with universal natural law, helping all and harming none. I welcome the presence of my highest vibrational ancestral guides and thank them for their help. I ask that I be protected fully during this process. I now enact the ancestral auric cleansing process using powerful vibrational waves and frequencies. It is done."

Feel your high-vibrational ancestors surround you. These could be beings that you've met in your lifetime or beings from very far back in your ancestral lines. These are often beings who lived as healers in their life as your ancestor, have incarnated as healers before, or specialize in healing from a spirit guide perspective.

Feel them surround you and sense each one of them begin to resonate out high-vibrational frequencies that are specifically calibrated to cleanse your aura. You can picture this the way you would picture sound waves interacting with a liquid. These waves will come into your aura and be the precise vibrational frequency to dislodge ancestral density from it. Feel these frequencies coming at you. You might perceive colors, lights, sounds, scents, or tastes. You might feel feelings or think words. Allow these frequencies to also clean and clear your physical body so your aura and your body get a complete ancestral cleansing.

Receive these frequencies and feel that move through you. Say thank you. When it feels complete, you can thank them and see yourself being refilled with pure white light coming out of the golden faucet above you. Then, continue with your day, making sure that you ground yourself and drink plenty of water. You can put a little untreated sea salt under your tongue to help integrate the cleansing.

Rewriting Encodement and Buffing the Inside of the Auric Shell

We talked in an earlier chapter about how there are imprints from the egg that you were made from and your mom's body that exists on the inside lining of the outer layer of your aura. In this clearing, we will cleanse that shell of all but the highest frequencies that serve your best and highest good.

Center yourself with some deep breathing and then repeat the following: "I ask that all that transpires during this clearing process be for the very highest good of all life and in accordance with universal natural law, helping all and harming none. I ask that whatever is for my highest and best interest will come through easily and gently and that I be protected fully during this process. I welcome my ancestral guides as well as the higher selves of my biological grandmother and mother. I also welcome all the archangels to assist with this clearing."

Feel all the guides that you just called in surround you. State the following: "I now enact the process to rewrite the encodement inside my auric shell and buff it out so it's clean and clear. I now ask the archangels to write new coding for me that personifies the highest frequencies, including joy, love, harmony, and prosperity."

Feel all these guides dispense a group of little elemental scrubbers. Feel them go into the inside layer of the outer shell of your aura and begin buffing off language, encoding, and density that no longer serves you. You may perceive sensations during this process—sounds, smells—you might have words or ideas, and you might feel feelings. You may feel fear, doubt in yourself, sadness—all kinds of emotions that are natural to being human but don't necessarily qualify as feeling good. Our goal in this book is to help move you into a space of feeling great all the time. When we remove these lower-frequency densities from your aura, it gives you more high-vibrational energy, and you are a human projector, so it creates a life of high vibration, and you get the opportunity to feel good all the time.

Feel all these little elemental scrubbers buffing, scrubbing, and erasing the old codes on the inside of your auric shell. Now, feel the archangels singing and pointing their voices and their energy at you. They are surrounding you with joy, love, light, and the most high-frequency customized personal energy for your optimal best life and health. Receive it. Repeat the word *yes* as the energetic sound waves penetrate your aura and rewrite all the coding, filling it with high-vibrational energy. Thank everybody involved. Make sure to drink plenty of water. Do some grounding activities today and make sure you're really in your body.

KEEPING
YOUR AURA
HEALTHY

Your electromagnetic fields are woven through your body and create your auric egg out around you. It is intensely connected to your physical health and vitality. The physical body that is visible to us and the electromagnetic parts of the physical body and its field that are not visible to us are all one unit. The aura is an intrinsic and essential part of the living organism. This is the case with every living thing on planet Earth, whether a plant or an animal. Many people also feel that with minerals and stones that have not been manipulated by humans.

As you recall, Earth herself is a living being whose body is the planet and her atmosphere is part of that body. She has an aura that consists of an electromagnetic field and an additional specific magnetic field. In this section, we will discuss health as it connects with the aura.

EFFECTS OF NON-NATIVE
EMFS ON YOUR AURA

We have been talking a lot in this book about electromagnetic fields (EMFs). Specifically, we have been talking about the fields that are generated by living things. That's why we have been calling them biofields. There is another type of electromagnetic field that you hear about frequently. It's the kind emitted from electronic devices that are made by humans. We refer to those as non-native EMFs.

While our human-generated biofields are full of energy and goodness, non-native EMFs are harmful to our health and our auras. They specifically affect our auras by interfering with them. They not only cause ill effects on our health, which we'll talk about a little more below, but also interfere with the way that the photons move through our bodies and our biological internal wiring. Non-native EMFs make that movement exist in less healthy states. They also lower our vibrational frequency.

Look at a beautiful bird outside on a tree. You can feel its frequency. Choose a songbird that is singing and looks like a delicate, beautiful living creature. You feel happy feelings and high-vibrational energy. It is so alive as it sings in the sun. Now, look at a microwave or a router or your phone. If anything, you might sense a lower vibration not synonymous with joy or health and instead synonymous with the plastics with which it's constructed.

Cell phones, tablets, computers, and home appliances, including microwave ovens, produce non-native electromagnetic fields/EMFs. The U.S. National Cancer Institute informs us that an electrical field is produced by voltage. As voltage increases, so does the electrical field.

One of the big differences between biofields and non-native electromagnetic fields is voltage. For biofields, the voltage that passes through our body is far lower, and our biological circuitry evolved to easily handle that quantity of voltage. The amount of voltage passing through devices (non-native EMFs) is higher, and our bodies are not equipped to be too close to that.

A magnetic field is the flow of current through an electrical device. According to the U.S. National Cancer Institute, electrical fields can be buffered by walls and other objects. In contrast, magnetic fields can pass through buildings, different materials, and even living things.

In 2017, a study by Magda Havas of Trent School of the Environment (Trent University) found evidence of cellular damage caused by non-ionizing radiation, which is emitted by cell phones, home appliances, Bluetooth-connected devices, microwave ovens, televisions, computers, Wi-Fi routers, cordless telephones, smart energy meters, and power lines. Havas's research highlighted that non-ionizing radiation interferes with the oxidative repair of our cells, which can lead to cancer as well as fatigue, mitochondrial dysfunction, and more.

A study of the effects of cell phones and other wireless devices on children was conducted by Anthony Miller and team in 2019 from Dalla Lana School of Public Health, University of Toronto. They discovered that a cell phone near a child's head exposes deep brain structures to greater radiation doses per unit of volume, including the skull's bone marrow, on a roughly 10-fold higher local dose than an adult would experience. This may be partially because children have thinner tissues and bones than adults. It's also because they are receiving the same amount of radiation but have smaller heads and brains than adults.

Plus, studies have shown that men keeping cell phones in their pockets are at risk of low sperm counts and impaired sperm motility. Non-native EMFs have been proven in numerous studies to be endocrine disruptors for both men and women.

We know that non-native EMFs are proven to disrupt our physical health. I believe they also have a significant effect on our auras. If you've ever walked under a big set of power lines or near a substation, think about how that feels. If you're sensitive, you almost feel the unpleasant, static-like tingling in your aura. I also feel it sometimes in my head. When our physical bodies experience disruption, that echoes out into our aura; it's important that we educate ourselves on the things we can do to prevent more harm. I discuss this more in depth in my book, *The Healing Home: A Room-by-Room Guide to Positive Vibes*. You can also check out Nick Pineault's and Dr. Joseph Mercola's books on the topic. The website of the Environmental Working Group is one of my favorite resources for these types of health topics, and they have a guide to safer cell phone use available on their website as well as a plethora of other helpful information.

You can measure EMFs in your environment with a gaussmeter by Meterk or TriField. Use it in the areas where you spend the most time. That means where you sleep, spend time in the evenings reading or watching television, and where you work, whether that's at your office or in your home office. Cell phones especially emit a certain kind of non-native electromagnetic field labeled radio frequency. It's also known as Radio Frequency-Electromagnetic Radiation (RF-EMR) and is referred to as microwave radiation.

Make sure to arrange your bedroom so you are sleeping in a low-EMF area. Do not spend time right next to your Wi-Fi router. Keep your phone away from your body when not in use, especially during sleep. Reduce phone use and use wired earbuds as opposed to Bluetooth wireless earbuds. This keeps the phone and any Bluetooth devices away from your brain, which is especially vulnerable to damage.

According to the U.S. National Cancer Institute, a distance of 12 to 20 inches from a computer screen has slightly lower radiation. Staying at least one foot away from most appliances is recommended. Original studies on early, lower-power cell phone models by the FCC (Federal Communications Commission) recommended maintaining a distance of at least one foot from all cell phones to avoid hazardous effects.

There are lots of EMF-blocking blankets on the market. They are a great idea if you sit with your laptop near your abdomen or in your lap frequently. They are often recommended for pregnant women to protect babies in utero. Use them to protect your internal organs. EMFs are endocrine system disruptors. They also disrupt the energy of those reproductive organs, which have their own biofield that generates a portion of the aura.

Keep non-native EMFs out of your aura as much as possible. Try to situate routers, power strips, and electronics as far away from areas where you spend the most time, like your workstation and bed. With a laptop, locate the router and printer on the other side of the room, far away from you. Try to place routers in the most unused area of the house. Unplug routers at night or check out the JRS Eco routers.

Reduce effects of non-native EMFs by unplugging devices and turning them off at night. Cell phone and Wi-Fi routers emit non-ionizing, non-native electromagnetic fields. Non-ionizing radiation is proven to cause brain cancer, emotional disorders, ADHD, and migraines. The WHO (World Health Organization) states that radiofrequency radiation is possibly carcinogenic to humans. The non-ionizing part is what makes them wireless. It means that wireless energy moving through your aura and body and affecting it. Distance can help reduce it.

Do your best to reduce your aura's exposure to non-native EMFs so that you can keep it strong and healthy.

HEALTHY HABITS FOR A VIBRANT AURA

Some important ways to keep your aura healthy include:

- **Stay fully hydrated.** When you are sure to consume plenty of water throughout the day, you keep your body and its electrical cells nice and plump and ready to move those photons through you in the most optimal and helpful way. That also is what powers your aura! There's a fabulous book that my longtime cranial osteopath, Dr. Loretta Guzzi, always recommends named *Your Body's Many Cries for Water.* It is aptly titled!

- **Consider adding trace mineral drops and untreated Celtic sea salt to your daily regimen.** This will help improve hydration levels and bolster biofield conductivity. Take your hydration to the next level and add molecules of these electrically conductive substances. This increases your vital life force by allowing more photons and electrons and electromagnetic energy to move through your

AURA ALCHEMY

body and system with ease. This electricity pumps your heart and powers your cognition and everything that happens in your body. It generates your auric field, which is your personal power and your personal space. Most people consuming a traditional American diet are grossly mineral deficient. The majority of our food is grown in soil that is minerally deficient due to industrial agriculture. Choosing to eat living food grown smaller-scale, locally, organically, and in soil that is rich with minerals can also assist this process.

- **Choose healthy, ideally organic, whole foods and avoid processed foods.** Processed foods contain almost no life force. They are dead. That is the case with industrially grown fruits and vegetables. When you eat foods that are alive and still contain energy and electromagnetic charge, you feel it. That can also be the case with ultrahigh quality, organic, lovingly, and humanely raised and cared-for animal products. If the animals are living in and existing in a natural, healthy environment that includes plenty of room to play and to be free and consume grasses and the healthy food that is close to what they would've consumed in the wild, then their life force remains energized and more intact. This also includes wild fish. When we consume dairy, eggs, meats, or other animal products that come from these types of conditions, as with all our food, we can thank the animals and plants that were involved in

162

nourishing us and receive that life force with gratitude. This is another way to empower your energy body, including your aura, to be healthy and full of vitality.

- **Spend time outdoors and limit exposure to non-native EMFs.** Electromagnetic frequencies exist throughout our bodies all the time. When those fields contact fields from human-made appliances and devices, things can go downhill. Non-native electromagnetic fields interfere with the optimal functioning of our physical body and our energy body. Reducing exposure makes a big difference. Increasing exposure to natural forms of light and energy powers up our aura. Sunlight, moonlight, even cloud cover, exposure to plants and animals, and time spent away from pavement and crowds and out in a natural environment empowers our energy body and our aura and invigorates us. That's why it feels good to go outside!

- **Spend time in the energy of feelings that you desire to experience, like joy and harmony.** What we pay attention to proliferates. When we focus on all the good-feeling situations, and live our lives to increase them, more goodness builds. The more that we feel good, the more wonderful we feel because these good feelings multiply. Choosing thoughts that feel good and situations that feel positive make a big difference in our lives. Think about when somebody is happy and smiling. Say they're outside in nature, they're with people they love, they're having fun laughing, and they're glowing, right? And then when somebody's inside in a dark room with no windows crunched over a computer with 10 devices around them, they look like a dim, low-energy, sallow-skinned being that is certainly not in possession of exuberant health. You have the power to make choices in each moment to increase your energy and empower your aura. Sometimes it takes effort. It takes a little bit of extra resolve to put down the device you're scrolling on and go outside for a walk after dinner and enjoy the sunset. It's worth it. The more you focus on that which feels good, the better you feel!

- **Pay attention to the environments in which you spend time and choose those that feel holistically good to you.** Be present to when you feel good and where you are at those times. Notice if fluorescent light, lots of non-native EMFs, too much pavement, crowded spaces, loud televisions blaring in restaurants, or things like that make you feel uneasy. Pay attention to where you feel good. Does that happen in certain people's homes or certain types of settings? What environments inspire you to feel comfortable, relaxed, and happy?

  Pay attention to the people with whom you spend time and make conscious choices and discern when you experience enhancement, neutrality, or harmful effects.

There are always certain people for each of us with whom we feel instantly relaxed and positive. Sometimes those people feel like soul family and sometimes they are new friends with whom we truly resonate. Identify those people and spend time with them. Ponder minimizing time with people that inspire the opposite. Choose and plan accordingly.

Take care of your body and make sure that you get plenty of high-quality deep sleep. Bolster this quality by removing non-native EMFs from your environment and unplugging appliances near the bed. Blue-blocking glasses do wonders after dark so that artificial light does not disrupt your circadian rhythm. Make it a priority to create a holistically healthy environment for yourself so you can feel wonderful all the time and therefore bolster your intuitive and psychic senses to use them to create the life of your dreams.

PART V

MANIFESTING WITH AURA ALCHEMY

In some ways, this section of the book is the most fun because we get to harness the massive power of alchemy in our auras and create a whole new world for ourselves! We are going to apply knowledge from particle physics to our auras. I'm going to share many years of shamanic insights and my personal theories and understanding through teaching shamanism to thousands of people and working with thousands of medical intuitive clients for 23 years. Understanding elementary particles and the mechanics of our auras and all the incredible energetic conditions that exist in our bodies and our world every day allows us to create our own alchemy.

The idea of alchemy originated in ancient history with Mesopotamian and Egyptian civilizations. Throughout the region at the time, there were different spiritual beliefs and rituals devoted to transformation. In essence, that's what alchemy is: transformation. Changing something into something else.

Alchemy was also the precursor to modern chemistry. Many alchemists during the Medieval and Renaissance periods endeavored to turn base metals into gold. Whether they succeeded at the time is unknown. There are reports of success not only in history but also later in scientific experimentation in the 1980s. Lawrence Principe was a scientific historian as well as a chemist at John Hopkins University at the time. He studied alchemical writings from the 17th century and created an experimental recipe to try to chemically construct what was termed a philosopher's tree. This was thought to grow forth alchemically from a seed of gold and then become the philosopher's stone, which was reported to turn base metals into gold. In a flask, he placed a mercury preparation and a lump of gold together. He then buried it in his lab in a heated sand bath. To his surprise after some time, the material had grown into a coral-like, branching tree of gold. He theorized that ancient alchemists were conducting chemistry experiments.

In this section of the book, we are going to manifest what we desire in our lives by using the power of transformation inherent in our auras, specifically when we work with them at a subatomic and elementary level. These particle waves and infinite fields that comprise all existence can be manipulated and influenced to do our bidding. Our intention is always the highest good of all life, helping all and harming none. And, with that intention, a pure heart, and a benevolent mind, we can create our own heaven on earth.

NEUTRINO AURA
MANIFESTATION

We create intentions through our thoughts and the fields that they create. These inner movements of photons in the body act like a projector and generate infinite fields and radiate out from us, creating the story of our lives. We are human projectors. We are radiant, and our energy, when in balance, is like an infinite spring bubbling forth from an inner source and radiating out into the universe. When it is time to exit the physical body, contraction occurs, and the energy goes back to the source. Then, the human exits the body and the radiation changes form.

When our intention is love, we elevate the frequency of the glue of all life. When that love is especially high vibrational, nonattached, unconditional, it can magnify the frequency of our intentions. That means when we deliver an intention with a big dose of healthy spiritual love, we empower it beyond measure.

As we learn to use our auric fields as a tool for healing, understanding, and manifestation, we will circle back to some of the shamanic concepts that we discussed earlier. In this section, we are working with shamanic retrieval as opposed to extraction. Retrieval simply means adding something to the being. It could be to the aura or the body or your life. It's simply adding as opposed to subtracting with extraction.

When we think about all the elementary particles that we've been making friends with and look at them in terms of manifestation, there are two standouts. One is photons, which make up the electromagnetic fields and force in our auras. They are some of the superstars of this book.

The other important and quirky supporting cast member is the neutrino. Neutrinos are a little bit zany, in my opinion. As someone who's been shamanically traversing alternate reality for more than 27 years, I have always thoroughly enjoyed my experiences with neutrinos.

In a shamanic journey with the archetypal magician figure Merlin as the guide, I posed a question that had been gnawing at me: can neutrinos carry thought forms or intentions? Merlin took me into a realm made of only neutrinos. The sensations and sensory experience were delightful. It felt like pure potentiality in a way. Then we went inside a singular neutrino. In the center, there was an endless well of emanating concentric circles that were all touching one another and were a source of pure energy and white light. It was divine source energy. Merlin showed me that is what powers neutrinos.

As you may remember, the unique nature of neutrinos extends to their lack of interaction with other fermions. That's why they pass through us and Earth at breathtaking speed, as if we're not even here. There are 400 billion neutrinos, primarily from the sun, passing through each of our bodies every single second. We exist in an infinite, constant cascade of high-velocity neutrinos.

For a long time, scientists believed neutrinos did not have any mass. They now know that they do have a very small amount of mass. That is why they are fermions as opposed to bosons, which are force and charge carriers. Instead they're something else, almost outliers within the system of fermions.

Merlin taught me that the infinite source energy within the neutrino center can be affected by the electromagnetic fields that are created by the movement of photons through the brain, also known as thought. We can direct neutrinos using those fields of electromagnetic energy/charge created by our thoughts. Every time a thought goes through our brains, it *is* the movement of photons through the circuitry of the brain and the body. Those photons, as you recall, create fields. And they're part of the composite of fields numerous moving photons in the body that create our aura or biofield.

When we have a thought, it emanates out from our brain and body through our aura. Each of our auras is submerged in the endless cascade of neutrinos that is happening through the entire Earth's atmosphere. Those neutrinos can be directed and affected by the fields that our thoughts create.

Next in my journey with Merlin, I met a guide that personified the neutrino. This being was like a little wizard or wizardess. It showed me how the neutrino was able to connect mystical Great Spirit source energy, comparable to what the Gnostics referred to as the great beyond, to the emanating electromagnetic fields created by the photons that move in our brains, thereby harnessing the energy of thought and creating alchemy.

This guide showed me that neutrinos exist in numerous dimensions. In our dimension, they interact with very few other particles. When they are intersected by our thought fields, they can bounce into other dimensions and imbue a different set of particles equivalent to fermions there with their energy. Then those fermion-like other-dimensional particles bounce them back eventually into our dimension. This dimension-hopping occurs because of a certain kind of angular momentum of the neutrino that is created by the thought field. Angular momentum is sometimes called spin by physicists. It's a bit of a misnomer, and it's a little more complicated, but you can think of it as something like that.

When the neutrino bounces back into our dimension and lands here, it initiates a change that began as thought form or field. Life is going in one direction, and neutrinos can intersect it and change its direction through this process.

So, a neutrino takes a thought form or intention that occurs in our brains from this dimension into one or more other dimensions, one of the infinite many. They end up in these other dimensions after they leave our auric field in this dimension. (In some cases, this may be a place outside of time, so it may appear as if no time has elapsed here after the process has transpired.)

When they interact with particles in that other dimension, they make some elements of our thoughts manifest there, meaning they interact with and change particles there. They pick up some influence in that way. It is a greater inclination to cause influence on fermions here.

Then, when they bounce back to our dimension, they have more weightiness, and they end up influencing matter and charge to create our intentions in this dimension. The fermion-like particles in the other dimension are, in a way, giving the neutrinos a little bit more intentional bulk.

It's not real mass or real bulk; it still allows the neutrino be lightweight, but it brings it into a frequency that can hold more form. Then our intention transmits an activation that ends up in this dimension. The process of thought form fields of photons passing near or thorough neutrinos can have an activating quality. It activates a change in the neutrino's angular momentum that initiates the rest of the process.

Neutrinos can be harnessed like little energetic thought form messengers. My guides showed me that all particles can technically carry human-generated thought forms and intentions. The Higgs boson carries such a strong vibration of its own that it doesn't have a lot of room for other frequencies, so it's less true for that particle.

My guides and I all tend to love paradoxes. In this journey, something I had learned in past journeys was reiterated: multiplicity is singularity and vice versa. A classic paradox. This idea of paradoxes is always exciting to me—that two seemingly opposite things can be true at the same time. In this paradoxical manner, we think of time as a strong, binding part of our lives. It's actually, according to the neutrino guides, a weaker force than we think it is, and it can be mastered. It can become nonexistent and be manipulated with certain quantum knowledge. In the journey, Merlin said we can do everything with time.

All people are emanations. We are radiating outward due to our auras and the fact that we're made of particles that are simply excitations of endless fields. We're connected to everything. We can harness the power of thought forms and neutrinos to bend time and space to our will.

Free will is also important. It's created in some ways by our thoughts. It's each individual's responsibility to choose, via our free will, to walk in integrity. When we walk in integrity, we're choosing a compassionate and benevolent detachment. In a way, that is also a force of unconditional universal love.

The glue of our dualistic dimensions is love. When its frequency is high, we see it and feel it in places like the angelic realms or dimensions. Many of us have felt that and experienced it through working with angel cards, meditation, feeling our spirit guides, and shamanism. Those higher-frequency dimensions have more charge and less matter. Here on Earth, we have diversity at this time in our evolution. We have some of those high-vibrational energies that are lighter. And we also have denser, lower frequencies that seem heavier and stickier. Karma has a sticky quality, and that's something I work with a lot with my medical intuitive clients. There is the dense, karmic glue that creates the process of incarnation and the passing on of ancestral density through generations. And, there is also the higher vibrational glue of all infinite dimensions from duality (the simultaneous existence of the dense with the light—a.k.a. Earth at this time) to the very highest realms, which is simply love.

APPRECIATION AND GRATITUDE IN THE AURIC FIELD

When we apply the good-feeling thought energy of appreciation and gratitude to the auric field, we also elevate its frequency and magnify our intentions. So, in the spirit of the law of attraction and the work of Esther and Jerry Hicks, if we send our intentions out into the infinite, numerous fields of existence infused with appreciation, gratitude, love, and let's throw in some joy for good measure, we elevate their frequency so much that as they intersect the neutrinos passing through our auras, they infuse them with all those frequencies and the frequency of our intentions generated by our thoughts. This process creates super-power neutrinos.

Through the movement of angular momentum, each neutrino is traveling on a vector. Angular momentum is considered a vector quantity, which means it has two properties: direction (the direction it is going) and magnitude (how quickly it moves). When our thought fields and waves move out into our auras and intersect with neutrinos, I believe they influence that angular momen- tum. And in fact, that is what bounces them, so to speak, into another dimension where they have their interaction with fermion-like particles. Then the neutrinos bounce back into our dimension, where they change the direction of life and existence. These tiny, quixotic particles can have a massive effect on our lives.

In the activities that we will embark on in the rest of the section of the book, we will create alchemy through our interaction with neutrinos and other particles. We will harness the power of our thoughts and our auric fields to create the conditions we desire for our lives and to affect change in our lives. We will always do this in utmost integrity and with the intention that everything we do is for the highest good of all life. That means accord- ing to universal natural law, as I was taught by my late medicine teacher, Laurie. It is helping all and harming none. You will see in our meditations and activities how we always infuse that intention. It protects us, but it also makes sure that we do not cause collateral damage as we tinker with the particles, waves, and fields that comprise our reality. Our reality intersects other realities, and our universal intention is raising frequency and vibration and perhaps being part of reducing and eventually eradicating suffering for all sentient beings and extending that same intention to the entirety of existence.

This process is absolutely meant to be fun! It is also not novel or a game with which to fool around. It's real life, for all life. It encompasses the physical, the nonphysical, and the undefinable. What a gift to expand our hearts, minds, and vision to witness and encompass an infinitely more intricate and benevolent reality than we ever imagined.

HOW TO CHARGE
YOUR AURA FOR
MANIFESTATION

I'm so happy that I've gotten to go on this journey with you through all the layers and types of waves and particles that comprise our auras of everything around us. It's been my honor to introduce you to elementary particles that comprise light in all its forms. To me, everything is alive, and these infinitesimally small particles are like familiar friends who are always near.

It's fun to share my observations as a medical intuitive combined with concepts from chemistry and particle physics to show how light in its wave and particle forms combine with resonances, which are more of an abstract phenomenon, to create our auras. These resonances may be created by our thoughts and a result of the movement of photons. The energy fields that surround us and all living things are truly multidimensional wonders.

All this background has now prepared you to use the power of your energy field to get whatever you want in life as long as it's for the highest good. We are going to talk now, even more than we did in our previous chapters, about the empty spaces between the photons that comprise your aura and the particles, waves, and resonant frequencies that are interacting with the aura. Energy fields and their components are all interwoven with empty space. So is everything in our multiverse. As you've learned, every star, every stone, every human, is primarily empty space. In this chapter, we are going to take some time to deeply understand and dive into the space between particles in our auric fields. That understanding allows us to harness our powers of manifestation most effectively.

Empty space is everywhere, in absolutely everything! It is a part of all matter. Let's use an ice cube as an example. It is made of frozen water. Let's imagine this is an ice cube made of distilled water, so there are no additional minerals in it. Just pure H_2O. So, this ice cube is made of many water molecules. An ice cube that is one cubic inch in size contains somewhere around five hundred sextillion H_2O molecules. It's a bit mind-boggling. In between each of these molecules, there is empty space. Plus, in each molecule, there are two hydrogen atoms and one oxygen atom, and those are also separated by empty space.

Let's look at one hydrogen atom from one molecule. That hydrogen atom has a nucleus at its center. The nucleus of the atom is made of protons and neutrons. Inside the nucleus, one proton and one neutron cluster together and spin around each other. There is a bit of empty space between them because they never actually touch. Protons and neutrons are both made up of hadrons. Hadrons are a type of particle that are made of two or three bundled, even smaller elementary particles called quarks that are held together with a strong nuclear force.

The nucleus of the atom is orbited by one tiny electron. This lone electron may be smaller than the proton and neutron, but it is mighty. This one electron moves so quickly that it forms a haze around the nucleus of the atom. It would look like an extremely thin, fog-like layer around the nucleus of the atom if we could see it.

Envision a golf ball in your mind. This golf ball is the nucleus of the atom. Picture the proton and neutron inside it about the size of small marbles. Imagine the golf ball inside a translucent basketball. The edge of the basketball is the electron haze made by that one tiny electron moving tremendously fast. Here's the catch: imagine that basketball is about 160 feet in diameter! Think about all that empty space between the golf ball nucleus and the outer shell of the basketball. The proportion of empty space to matter and energy is striking. There is so much empty space with which we can play and manifest.

We are starting to grasp the magnitude of empty space in the universe and our bodies. Now, let's think some more about our auras. We will look one more time at our friend the single hydrogen atom. Imagine it is transported to a nuclear reactor. There it is hurled through space at incredible speed to crash into other hydrogen atoms. This liberates energy that is made of electrons. So, it splits off the electron of our hydrogen friend and lets it loose. This is called nuclear fission, which is separating atomic particles to liberate energy. In the case of generating nuclear energy in power plants, it is collected.

Our sun is powered by nuclear fusion, which would make our hydrogen friend collide with another hydrogen atom, and they would split apart and partially fuse to become a helium atom, which is heavier than a hydrogen atom. That liberates a large quantity of energy and powers the sun. If the liberated electrons jump to an outer orbital of the electron cloud, they use energy. But if they jump to an inner orbital, they give up energy. This energy is released as a tiny packet of light energy, or a photon.

Photons make up light and our auras. Even in our auras, the empty space echoes and is multitudinous. The photons in our auras are not the only thing in that bubble of space around us. We have air, neutrinos, and whatever else is near.

So, what do we do with all this empty space? We fill it with exactly what we want and desire. In a few minutes, I'm going to take you on a journey into your own aura. We are going to experience some of these waves, particles, and resonances that comprise your aura and get to know them and feel their essences.

Then, we are going to go into the spaces between to experience them on a visceral level. When you're able to have an internal and instinctive experience of the spaces between the particles in your aura, you will get a profound sense of that empty space. It is primarily neutral. Your auric energy field is also woven through your physical body and that, combined with your aura, shares a snapshot into the frequencies that are comprising your individual field of manifestation energy and more. Knowledge is power, especially in this case. If we have knowledge of the frequencies that are projecting outward from our being creating our reality, because we're a human projector, then we have the power to change them.

I'd love for you to take a moment and reflect before we begin our meditation experience on what frequency you want to place in the empty space of your aura. Consider that and think about what you want in your life. A lot of times we don't know what that is, even when we think we do. It is a powerful practice to reflect on what you want at night before bed. Or, in the morning when you wake up, take a few minutes in your journal and reflect on what you desire and therefore what you are going to draw to you.

Then, come back to the central question of what frequency to place in the spaces between the particles, waves, and resonances in your being. This is going to be your primary frequency. I'll share some examples that you might choose. These are a suggested menu, but you can expand on them and choose whatever you desire and change it as well. You might use unconditional love, joyful wealth, happiness and harmony, high-vibrational energy, pure joy, boundless expansion, elevated consciousness, victory and light, ecstatic dancing, or abundant success.

Settle on one frequency for this exercise. You can do this exercise as often as you desire. You can change the intention to different frequencies and power the empty space in your being with diverse energies.

SUPERCHARGE YOUR EMPTY SPACE GUIDED PROCESS

You'll do most this process with your eyes closed, so read it first and then review it, closing your eyes in between as you can. Make sure you have your journal handy in case you want to take any notes about your experience.

Get comfortable and make sure your body is fully supported. Close your eyes and take three deep cleansing breaths, dropping into your physical body. If you need more time, practice some mindful deep breathing for a while.

Bring your awareness to your brow center, right between your eyebrows. That's the seat of your inner seeing, second to the center of your chest. If you would prefer to bring your awareness to the center of your chest, you can also do that.

Get present there and feel the totality of your awareness in this area. Now, from this centered space, expand your awareness out in front of you through your auric field, so it'll either be in front of your forehead or in front of your upper chest.

As you bring this awareness out and through, feel it expanding outward. Next, simultaneously feel your focus refine and come to a smaller and smaller point in your auric field about one foot in front of you. As you get to a smaller point, begin to notice elementary particles like electrons and photons, waves of energy and light on various free frequencies and wavelengths, and resonances that you may experience like moving ripples through your auric field. Just notice with no judgment or desire to influence.

Notice how these particles, waves, and resonances feel. Are there more of some than others? Bring your focus to an even smaller space in your aura in front of you and begin to hone in on the space between one or more particles, wavelengths, or resonances. Find that empty space. You may feel like you are gently squeezing your awareness in front of your forehead to focus and find the space between. The energy is always moving, and you can allow it to slow down so the empty space stays stationary in your mind's eye.

Be in this empty space. Feel like you're standing there in a miniaturized form of yourself. Bring your awareness there and look around your aura. You have paused your vision of your aura so you can inspect it. You may see particles, waves, and resonances suspended around you. Notice them and their light, frequency, and color. Do they give you a certain mood or flavor? Notice the textural elements we talked about past chapters. Then bring your attention to this empty space where you're standing in miniature and feel its openness.

Expand your awareness through the empty space. You are in the individual energy field of your consciousness within your own aura. Feel your whole aura now by expanding your awareness and consciousness. Feel the oval-shaped bubble of your aura peppered with empty space around you. Keep your focus on the vast amount of empty space and stay focused on that openness.

Now, bring your attention to the word or phrase that you selected at the beginning of the exercise. I will use *joyful wealth* as our example in this exercise, but use whatever you've chosen.

Repeat your word or phrase aloud to yourself as you feel the energy field of your awareness inside the empty space, stating it multiple times: joyful wealth, joyful wealth, joyful wealth. Say it into the empty space. Sense the open emptiness and say the words more. Seed the intention in the openness. Keep doing that for a few minutes, infusing it and your whole aura.

Further multiply it through all the empty space in your aura. State aloud, "Multiply joyful wealth (or your intention) through all empty space in my auric field, body, and energy body. Proliferate now." Repeat the phrase yourself as you feel it infuse the bubble of light around you and your entire physical body, repeating it over and over like a mantra.

Now, use an affirmative statement to embody it, like: "I am joyful wealth." Or, whatever phrase or frequency you've chosen. You are embodying this frequency now.

Next, state aloud, "It is done." You have now planted this frequency in that space.

Rest in it and notice what it feels like. Use some of the techniques that we talked about in previous chapters as far as noticing textures and frequencies of auras. Is there a sense of taste, color, or feeling?

Your sense of it may be mutable because your chosen frequency may contain many smaller frequencies. As you know, we discussed in previous chapters that a larger frequency can hold many smaller strands of frequency, and we've seen that in our auras and bodies as well as in other people and out in nature. This is the case with the frequencies in many auras. You may notice and experience on a deep instinctive level what this frequency you just seated feels like as you sense into your aura.

When you're ready, bring your awareness back to your physical body, keeping your eyes closed, returning your focus to either your brow center or the center of your chest. Feel the pulsing of your awareness there and notice that it is pulsing the frequency that you just instilled. So, if you bring your awareness to the center of your chest, you should feel your intention pulsing there. Move your awareness to your brow center, feeling your intention pulsing there. You can also bring your awareness to your abdomen and feel the essence of your intention pulsing there. Observe the bottoms of your feet and notice that they are pulsing your intention. Move your consciousness to the palms of your hands to feel your intention there. Now, use your awareness like you've learned in other chapters to feel the full entirety of space that comprises your entire aura all around you; feel out to the edges of your aura and feel how the entire thing is pulsing with the frequency of your intention.

You *are* the frequency you have chosen. You and it are now the same being. Each frequency could be personified as a being because everything is alive. Everything exists in whatever way we choose to perceive it. So, embody your frequency and become that being who exists in the frequency you have intended. You are a human projector, and now you are creating a reality infused with your conscious intention.

AURA MANIFESTATION MEDITATIONS AND PROCESSES

In the following aura manifestation processes, you will use your knowledge and intention to create circumstances, conditions, and high-vibrational energy for yourself. We'll be applying all the concepts that we went over here in the book to different areas of life.

Before Each Process

Before you undertake each of these processes, do some deep breathing and center yourself. Then you can dive in and use the invocation for each process and enact it, knowing that your body and energy field is relaxed and prepared to receive all its goodness.

After Each Process

After you complete each of these processes, make sure you drink plenty of water. Make sure you feel totally present to yourself and ground yourself in your five senses before you continue going about your day. It can be a good idea to place a few granules of Celtic sea salt under your tongue or in your water to help ground you and encourage excellent electrical conduction in your body.

"BEAUTY IS IN ME" MEDITATION

State the following invocation aloud or in your mind: "I ask that all that transpires during the entirety of this meditation process be for the very highest good of all life and in accordance with the universal natural law, helping all and harming none. I ask that whatever is for my highest and best interest to come through easily and gently and that I be protected fully during this process. I welcome the presence of my highest vibrational guides, guards, and teams and thank them for their help."

Next, say this: "I invoke the power of beauty to fill my aura and body. I appreciate the beauty in my life. I allow my life and experiences to illustrate the beauty of the world. I understand that beauty is a sensory offering of delight, and it inspires gratitude and appreciation. Beauty helps me live in the present moment. Beauty is within me."

Bring your attention to your auric egg. Feel its edges. Take a minute and sense the whole space around you. In a moment, you are going to conjure a thought form symbolizing beauty to you personally. You'll be thinking about it and directing it out into your aura and inviting it to make contact with some of the neutrinos moving through your aura. This image and thought of beauty that you will immerse yourself in will generate a strong enough field to affect the angular momentum of some of those neutrinos and help bounce them out into a different dimension. Then they'll get bounced back into this dimension to bring even more beauty to your life. This will change the direction of your life from the one in which it's traveling to one with more beauty and more high vibration.

So, take the time to allow yourself to be filled with an image that embodies beauty for you. It could be flowers that are colorful and in bloom and have a delightful scent and perhaps some friendly bees buzzing if that would bring a nice auditory component to you. Or maybe you can add an experience of the sensation of a warm breeze and sunshine on your skin as you're having a sensory experience of appreciating the beauty of these flowers. Or, add something comparably splendid for you, like listening to a piece of music or looking at a piece of art. Make sure whatever you choose embodies a high-vibrational frequency. This is not the time to go avant-garde or edgy.

Focus in on that essence of beauty. Picture it. Choose a word to describe how it feels and repeat the word as needed to yourself. Visualize the scene and say something to yourself like, "I'm so grateful and appreciative that I get to experience such beauty. I am blessed." As you fill your senses with these sensations and these words, say, "Beauty is in me; it's radiating out from me. And it's raining out through my aura and making contact with the perfect neutrinos who shall manifest beauty in my life. Beauty is in me. I am beauty."

Feel it radiate out from you and see if you can sense the neutrinos as they move out of your aura into another dimension and likely pop right back in and affect the change. You can notice if there's any time lapse in this process.

CHOOSING VIBRANCY AND COLORS MEDITATION

To begin, say to yourself or aloud, "I ask that all that transpires in this vibrancy and colors meditation be for the very highest good of all life and in accordance with the universal natural law. I ask that I be surrounded by the full spectrum of all color in its highest vibrational states. I ask that this prismatic bestowal of multifaceted energy filled my aura and surround me. I ask that it protect me and raise my frequency so that I may soar to new heights while remaining rooted in my body and manifesting exactly what I desire for the highest good. I welcome the presence of color vibration and all the high-vibrational color guides that would like to work with me. Thank for your help."

Sense the space around you and the edges of your aura. Invoke a cascade of color to fill you by inviting the Greek goddess Iris to be with you. State aloud or internally, "Dearest Iris, please join me now and receive my deepest gratitude. Please wrap me in the rainbow of all color and help me receive all the color frequencies that are for my highest good to heal me, delight me, bring me joy, help me realize my heart's desires, and align me with my life's purpose. Thank you."

Envision Iris before you. Reach out and hold spirit hands with her. Feel her aura and her hands pumping the full magnitude of color vibration into your being. It is everything that is for your highest good, magnified just for you. These colors will raise your frequency on every level. They will heal, repair, and enliven the mitochondria in your cells. Now, feel the rays of colored light filling your auric egg and allow yourself to receive all that is for your highest good by saying the word *yes*, like a mantra. Perceive the colors in your aura. Close your eyes for a while and receive and perceive. When you're done, make some notes or—even better—create some colorful art.

AURIC ROTATION OF CONSCIOUSNESS MEDITATION

This meditation is similar, in part, to the practice of yoga nidra that involves rotation of consciousness. Usually in yoga nidra, we move our awareness and consciousness through various parts of the physical body. In this case, we're going to do the same thing with our aura. When we do this in the body, it brings energy and awareness to these parts of the body and allows it to receive spontaneous healing in what yogis refer to as the fourth state, which is synonymous with yogic sleep and deep restoration. Our process will be similar but also a little bit different. Let's get started!

State internally or aloud, "I ask that all that transpires during this rotation of consciousness meditation be for the very highest good of all life and in accordance with universal natural law, helping all and harming none. I ask that it fill me with joy, golden light, and high-vibrational happiness. Thank you."

Bring your attention to the very top of your aura three feet above your head. Feel that area of your aura. Sense it pulsing. Next, guide your attention down and around the edge of your aura out in front of your upper chest. Feel that place gently vibrate. Move your awareness down the front of your aura on the edge of the shell to right in front of your knees. Inhabit your awareness in that part of your auric eggshell. Cycle your attention down three feet below your feet, on the bottom edge of your aura. Sense that space and feel the roots of your body growing through that and down into the center of the earth.

Propel your awareness up behind you directly across from the front of the knees. Point and feel your attention there. Next, take it up directly across from your center of your chest behind you and feel your awareness there. Bring it back up to the top of your aura.

Next, you will sense sections of your whole aura. You'll feel from the inner edge of the shell, all the way in to where it meets your physical body. Begin at the top of your aura and come all the way down the left side of your body to the halfway point of your aura. So, you'll be feeling the top left 25 percent of your aura. Sense that whole space and feel it pulsate. Rotate your consciousness down and feel the bottom left 25 percent of your aura. Feel that area tingle. Next, bring your attention to the bottom right 25 percent of your aura. Feel its essence. Lastly, bring your awareness to the top right 25 percent of your aura. Feel it resonating. Now, notice all four of those quadrants simultaneously. Envision them all being filled with golden, radiant light. Your aura is pulsing with high-vibrational golden light. Perceive how warm and relaxing it is. Embody how blissful and content it is. Experience how you're connected to your entire aura and how it strong is. It is golden, pulsing, and you are one with the universe. This is a great meditation to do before sleep.

APPRECIATING AURIC ABUNDANCE TO INVOKE WEALTH

In this process, we are going to use the power of appreciation and good feelings and thoughts to bring abundance and wealth into our lives. I read something recently that reframed the idea of overwhelm in terms of abundance. It said that sometimes when we feel overwhelmed, it is simply that we need to expand our capacity for abundance. I like that. As we move into this process, where we will be specifically invoking wealth and opening to high-vibrational abundance for our highest good, it can be a great concept to keep in mind. Another aspect of abundance is having the resources, skills, and knowledge to be able to energetically navigate the proliferation of good things in our lives. We will also be drawing wealth energy into the aura and allowing it to be seated in your being so that you can effortlessly live in that state, and your outer world will respond accordingly.

To begin, state internally or aloud, "I ask that all that transpires in the entirety of this process I am about to undertake be for the very highest good of all life and in accordance with universal natural law, helping all and harming none. I invoke the energy of affluence, abundance, and wealth into my aura and being for all time. I appreciate all the wonderful, abundant, prosperous experiences, energy, conditions, and resources that filled my existence. I am so happy that I'm so abundant, and I am so thankful that I am so wealthy. My affluence allows me to experience the spontaneous fulfillment of my desires. I appreciate that I get to live in a state of bliss, joy, and enjoyment of all that life has to offer. I'm thankful that I get to share my abundance with so many people and beings. It is such a joy to be a conduit for money. I feel such delight to be a conduit for affluence. I am so pleased to be a conduit for money, wealth, prosperity, and good feelings. Abundance blesses my life, and I share my blessings with great joy. It is done."

Now, you will empower your intention using the power of your thought waves, which are created by the movement of photons in your brain and body. They are creating fields that are resonating through your aura. We'll allow these fields to influence the angular momentum of the neutrinos (and other elementary particles) in your auric field so that they can may contact with the perfect interdimensional environments to bring back your intention and exponentially amplify and deposit it into your life, like a continual, massive, joyful deposit in your bank account. So it shall be.

Feel the edges of your auric egg with your awareness. You've gotten so good at it from all the practice we've been doing! Keep focusing on your awareness of that edge and the space between your body and that edge. Concentrate on that. Hold that awareness and then bring another piece of your awareness into the approximate center of your brain. From that center, feel and think the words *joyful wealth* and *blissful affluence*. Repeat those words and sense them emanating out from your brain as those photons create the field associated, and then use your intention to propel those vibrational frequencies out from your brain in a voluminous continual wave reaching all the way through your aura and out to that edge of your auric egg of which you've been holding awareness.

Feel like you have a continual spring of the words *joyful wealth* and *blissful affluence* bubbling out of the center of your brain, releasing more and more photons with more and more infinite fields and waves that are filling your entire aura. See your entire aura filled with this essence of "joyful wealth" and "blissful affluence." As your aura fills, see it overflow with those essences as they extend out around you. Notice how the edge of your auric egg, like we talked about in the past, is not finite, so its diffused edge particles are also infused with the essence that you've created. And so, it reaches out through this dimension.

You can simply notice. You need to do nothing to make the essence with which you filled your aura make contact with those neutrinos. This is naturally meant to happen, to affect their angular momentum and propel them out to numerous other dimensions and then allow them to snap back in to yours and upgrade your life. State the following aloud or internally, "I allow this energy of joyful wealth and blissful affluence to flow through my brain, body, aura, and life for all time, and I thank the neutrinos that made it possible and have changed the direction of my life into one of even more joyful wealth and blissful affluence. Thank you. It is done."

HEAL AND MEND THE AURA MEDITATION

In pop culture, you hear about dramatic things like ripped and torn auras with holes in them. These are alarmist! There's no way for there to be a rip or a hole in your aura. There's no way for it to be torn. It's simply a composite of the numerous fields within your body creating an electromagnetic field around you. What can be variable in your aura is the degree to which you fill it with your presence. You can infuse your being into your aura with a few different things that are not exclusive, and it can be a mixture of divine light energy, your unique individual essence, and other specific frequencies, whether it's divine feminine energy, masculine sacred energy, a combination of the yin and the yang, different qualities to the aura, and so on. When you take ownership and awareness of your aura consciously, then you strengthen it. If you wanted to experience a high-vibrational frequency, then you need to embody and fill your aura with more quantity of that frequency. In this activity, where we will heal and mend the aura, what we're doing is raising its frequency and empowering it to exist within the frequency of optimum health and radiant vitality. When you tap in to the endless flow of high-vibrational energy available to you, you can use it to enliven and almost metaphorically fluff up your aura and make it sparkly and beautiful.

To begin, state the following internally or aloud: "I ask all that transpires in the entirety of this meditation and process be for the very highest good of all life and in accordance with universal natural law, helping all and harming none. I ask that I be protected fully during this process, and I welcome the presence of my highest vibrational guides, guards, and teams and thank them for their help. My entire aura shall be easily and gently healed, mended, and drenched in high-vibrational joy and source energy. I allow myself to anchor my unique essence into my aura. This combination of high-frequency energy and my individual, unique essence has now created spontaneous fulfillment of my desires and joyful embodiment of my life's purpose. This is my reality, and I allow it to infuse me, my aura, my life, and existence for the highest good of all life. It is done."

Feel your spirit guides create a circle around you about 10 feet out from where your body is centered within it. Thank them. See your spirit guides, also known as your spirit family, with their energetic hands, palms out facing toward you. They are beaming the highest vibrational energy possible to you and your aura. Accept it by saying the word *yes*. Feel it bolster your individual essence and raise your frequency. See the space that fills your aura pulsing with this high-vibrational light. Watch it wave and shimmer. Sense your individual essence permeating out from the center of your chest, solar plexus, and/or abdomen. Watch your essence roll out, mixed in with these waves and shimmers of high frequency. It may look like colorful paint being swished through water. See how your individual essence meets this high-vibrational energy. Let yourself perceive it with your eyes closed and state aloud, "I am. I am." You can also say, "I am," and then your name. You could also say, "I am me." Feel your unique essence and affirm it by stating "I am me" or any of these phrases. Feel your quintessence filling your aura and the high-vibrational energy within it. Notice how your aura is pure, clear, and radiant. Notice how its edges are appropriately defined and your boundaries are healthy and that you're also beautifully, gently interconnected with all life in a way that is only for your highest good. Rest in this knowing and understanding and feel the love of your spirit family. Connect with them now and sense their auras and their energy. Notice the loving union of all life.

LOVE FOUNTAIN MEDITATION

In this meditation, you will be stepping into your true nature. Sometimes, we get separated from the reality of who we are. We are all fountains of the love eternally springing from a benevolent, neutral source. The essence of source energy is nonattachment. When we can tap in to that and open our hearts using our human body, we can touch the Divine. This occurs partly through the movement of photons and many other mechanisms to create chemical reaction that results in our experience of emotion. We can combine our benevolent neutrality with our ability to experience deep unconditional love that feels heart opening and heart expanding. This kind of love fills our beings and auras with its essence.

We have an incredible privilege being incarnated in human bodies that can experience emotions generated by the complicated symphony of neurotransmitters in our brains. We experience duality in this universe in a unique way because of our poignant and emotive nature. We can harness that tendency and elevate it so we can radiate unconditional love with no effort on our part beyond intention. We can utilize the power of our aura to do this.

Feel into what some would call your heart space. You can feel it as an abstract essence of your feeling nature, or you can sense it located physically in your body where it feels most present. For a lot of people, this will be the center of the chest.

Delve into your heart space. Notice how you perceive it. Bring your attention to humanity. Choose to do this affirmatively and hopefully. Think about the loving intention you would hold for people on Earth and all life. It might be something like, "Peace on earth and in the universe and joyful abundance for all life." If it were up to you, what would you intend for all beings?

Feel that and get a sense of it. By sharing that benevolent intention with the world, to hopefully raise its frequency, you can become a fountain of love and allow your aura to facilitate this with complete ease.

Bring your attention to the center of your chest or wherever you feel your loving center. State internally or aloud, "I ask that all that transpires during the entirety of this meditation process be for the very highest good of all life and in accordance with universal natural law, helping all and harming none. I ask that I be protected fully during this process, and I welcome the presence of my highest vibrational guides, guards, and teams. I offer my love and positive intention to all sentient beings that all may be enhanced."

Feel that love center within you. Focus on the essence of love. Immerse yourself in the word *love*. You can add nonattachment to make it more neutral, as needed. Conjure the feeling for yourself. You may think about a beloved pet or your child or someone for whom you feel positive and unconditional love of great magnitude. Repeat that word *love* in your mind. Envision the fountain of love that already exists within you. You might see it like an iridescent pink, shimmering fountain endlessly bubbling forth in the center of your being, cascading through your body and filling your aura.

Repeat the word *love* and see and feel its essence filling your being. Let it fill your aura all the way out into the far reaches of it. The whole auric egg is completely filled with endlessly bubbling love. Watch it begin to stretch out around you in the long, light strands of diffused echoes of particles that are your aura's edge and beyond. They reach out as luminous, minuscule tendrils into your world.

Offer your love to the world from a place of being filled. Love is free. Love transcends space and time. Love does not require physical proximity.

PART VI

TOGETHERNESS

In this section, we are going to discuss what happens when you put one or more auras together in one space. Our auras or composite electromagnetic fields are imbued with our essences to varying degrees. They often contain energies and frequencies associated with what we are experiencing. When we contact other people's auras, we may experience effects.

As an empath and intuitive, I am especially aware of the repercussions of interacting with other people's fields. Many of these effects are wonderful! They contribute to having fun, enjoying life, feeling like we belong to a community, and much more.

In my work as a medical intuitive, whether in person or remote, it's part of my job to connect with and interact with the clients' energy bodies, which includes their auras and all the electromagnetic fields that they produce. Oftentimes, I need to read that energy and synthesize the information to help find the root of discomfort or facilitate karmic or ancestral healing among many other things.

Let's jump in with both feet and learn how to best navigate interacting with other electromagnetic fields, how to protect ourselves, and fully enjoy our experience of being human.

WHEN AURAS INTERACT

Let's first talk about the overall experience of having more than one person in a space. From an electromagnetic perspective, it introduces one or more auric field imbued with consciousness. When one or more auras overlap, they create a combined field.

Electromagnetic fields are partially powered by the person's thoughts, emotions, and belief systems. When we insert our conscious awareness into any electromagnetic field, we affect it. As you know, our thoughts influence the movement and mechanics of the photons that create the aura, and in turn, those photons end up influencing our lives through the phenomenon of neutrino dimension-hopping that the spirit guide Merlin shared with us earlier.

When we are in proximity to other people, we can experience effects. Those effects can begin even at a distance. Earlier in the book, we discussed the possibility of telepathy particles, which is the phenomena of how somebody can think a thought and send it to another person nonphysically, and it can be received. We know that thought is intrinsically part of the movement of photons in the brain and aura. And we know that electromagnetic energy has effects on the quantum world.

Aura-to-aura effects occur before we're even in nearness sometimes. When we enter proximity with another person, even more happens. Each person has their auric egg radiating out around them about three feet in all directions. Remember, the edges of that egg are paradoxically finite and infinite. There is a definite edge with which we can work. We learned in previous chapters that there is coding etched into the inside of that bubble. But, conversely, we also learned there is still an infinite diffusion of particles extending out that facilitates our interconnection with all that exists.

When we get into closer proximity where auric egg bubbles begin to intersect, more effect occurs. In those cases, if we are in tune with the person, that often means that the interaction of these electromagnetic fields is occurring harmoniously. Another way to explain it is when you're in the presence of someone with whom you feel comfortable and have good feelings, that likely means that when those auras interact and inhabit the same space at the same time, there is a positive resonance.

There could be lots of reasons for this. It might mean that the flavor of thoughts that enliven both auras are aligned. It could also indicate that there is a complementary emotional resonance between the people. In the best of cases, it informs us that both people are aligned with good-feeling thoughts and are in a complementary state of consciousness with one another and through the interaction of their auras.

That might look like two people at a coffee shop having a conversation where they feel very in sync. It could look like a parent and child enjoying cuddle time and reading a book together. It's could appear as a couple hiking in nature and feeling like a cohesive unit while also feeling secure in their individuality.

When auras of living beings inhabit the same space, connection occurs. When our personal space (which is our aura) is impacted by other people, we have lots of tools to make that result positive. That's a big part of what we will discuss in the subsequent chapters in this section.

You can test this by doing a conscious experiment with somebody. Ideally, let them know what you're up to so they can participate. Begin as far apart as you can and move toward one another slowly so you can stop periodically and notice how you feel. As you get closer, try to notice the point where that relatively defined edge of each of your auric eggs begins to inhabit the same space. Take a moment to notice and feel. Move slightly closer so at least half of each of your auric fields are inhabiting the same space. Take turns being in neutrality and thinking about a situation or a feeling and notice through observation and sensing what happens and how the fact that your auras are intersecting effects this process. Do some experimentation!

When you are out in the world interacting with people, you can notice when your aura is overlapping somebody else's. Perhaps you're getting a cup of tea, and the barista is handing it over the counter to you. There will be some auric overlap there. How does it feel? You don't need to look at the other person; it's more about noticing the space that is simultaneously inhabited by two auras. Enjoy this observation process. Next, we will begin to look at how we can harness this knowledge to better our lives.

RADIANT MEETING GUIDED PROCESS

You can use the following process for any interaction. We're going to tailor it to a meeting that you would have in a professional context. But you can use these techniques wherever they feel most useful. This would work well for a job interview. It would work well to explore a business collaboration. It would work well if you're interviewing a new dog trainer or nanny.

If you're able, prepare for the process by centering yourself and doing some deep breathing. If it happens spontaneously, consciously take even a moment to bring yourself to your sense of being rooted in the present moment. A big part of this activity is noticing. It's kind of like the active listening of auric interaction. Set the intention that everything that transpires in the interaction be for the very highest good of all life. Sometimes, you might not have a chance to go through a full invocation. You can even quickly think something like "highest good of all" and let that infuse your aura and being.

When you enter the situation, take some time to notice the area where your two (or more) auras are overlapping. If you know that this meeting will be coming up, you can practice noticing overlapping auras so you're already prepared.

As you are a talking, place a little bit of your awareness on that auric area. If you have a desire to infuse the interaction with more harmony or understanding of each other's positions, you can use a single word to symbolize it. Or, use *joy* if you'd like to raise the frequency.

Then take that word and picture it in your mind. Give it a color that makes sense and make sure everything is in a high-vibrational, positive space. See that word in your brain. Know that it is infusing your electromagnetic fields at this time. Send it out through your aura effortlessly and know that it's influencing the angular momentum of the neutrinos in your aura to positively affect your aura and the aura of the other person.

Instantly, the energy of the word that you chose will start to affect the part of your aura that is overlapping with the other person. Watch the results of that in the other person's aura. Don't have any preconceived notions on how it will land.

Now is your time for active auric listening. Be tuned in to the aura effects and other nonverbal cues, like their body language, facial expression, and tone to help you understand how it landed. If you sent an energy like harmony and it appeared to provoke more resistance, then you might want to next try something like peace or serenity. If you sent an energy like joy and they started to open up and share more, then you might want to leave it at that and allow it to unfold.

This does require some multitasking! It's good to practice this with a friend or someone who knows what you're doing beforehand so when it comes up in a life situation you are ready. If you don't get a chance to do that, it's okay. Just listen to your heart and focus on benevolent neutrality and the affluence that you are creating in your life, which allows the spontaneous fulfillment of your desires and a high-vibrational life for the highest good.

After the interaction is concluded, make sure you thank the higher self of the person with whom you interacted. And if it's appropriate, you can even verbally thank them in the conversation and let the energy of appreciation and gratitude infuse both of your auras.

MAKING DIFFICULT CONVERSATIONS EASIER GUIDED PROCESS

Our next process is useful when you need to have a challenging conversation with someone. We always respect another's free will. As we operate in integrity, we take full responsibility for ourselves, our auric energy, and our behavior, and we allow our life to exist in a high-frequency state. When other people are not aligned with our state anymore, sometimes they will have less interaction with us and our lives. And that's okay. When you are aligning with the spontaneous fulfillment of your desires and your highest energy, you can be in that flow and allow your life to elevate.

As always, take some time to center yourself. Be sure that you infuse the interaction with the intention that everything that transpires be for the very highest good of all life and in accordance with universal natural law, helping all and harming none. Depending on the situation, you might be able to do this beforehand, but if not, then just do it in the moment.

As you enter the interaction, set an intention to be fully present. Know that energy of your thoughts will infuse your aura and the neutrinos passing through it and cause the desired effect. Choose something that embodies the outcome you'd like to create. Some examples might be if you are discussing divorce with a partner, you might want to have the conscious uncoupling process be infused with love, care, and kindness. With most situations, it's also helpful to add high-vibrational energy. The word *joy* is wonderful for doing so. Even though that might seem a little counterintuitive to discussion of divorce, if you did infuse it with joy, it would raise its frequency.

If you are having a conversation with someone with whom you have to terminate employment, you might want to infuse the interaction with caring and positive expectations for all as well as the ease of letting go.

When things change and people experience loss, or perceive that they might, sometimes they go into contraction and constriction. That is generally not a good-feeling state. If you are able to stay in a good-feeling state and use the energy of your thoughts to infuse your aura with that, then your much more likely to stay in neutrality or expansion, which are both positive states in which to remain.

Have a high-vibrational intention in mind as you have the conversation. Make sure that you return to it, repeating it internally like a mantra periodically. You'll focus on the conversation and the person, and then you'll quickly pop your attention to your intention. That might look like thinking the words *kindness* and *joy* as you have the conversation.

As you return your mental focus, albeit quickly, to your primary intention and good feelings thoughts, they echo out through the movement of photons in your aura. They infuse your aura with that energy. There may be a lot of other feelings swirling and occurring at that time. Those can infuse your aura too, and that's okay. It's important to feel our feelings and be in as little attachment to them as possible. If you are the one receiving the news of separation or job termination, you likely feel emotion that we might categorize as unpleasant.

It's totally normal, and we want to allow it to move through. If that is occurring, a great thing to do, if you are able to do so quickly in the moment, is to direct it down and into the earth. Allow the earth to receive that emotional energy because she has the ability to transmute it back into pure white light and use it for fuel. That lets you continually cycle the emotion out as you interject your positive emotional state through your intention, letting the interaction unfold as best as it can.

Take some time after it's complete when you're alone to journal about it. Let your thoughts and feelings flow, and release that which doesn't feel good to return yourself as easily as possible to good-feeling states of being. When you experience things that feel good, make sure to fully embody them and have them fill your aura. That helps you keep radiating that frequency so your life trajectory can raise vibration continually over time. That is conscious evolution. You have that power, and in each moment, you can choose consciousness and awareness to evolve as you desire.

GROUP SETTINGS WITH MANY AURAS IN ONE SPACE

As an empath and highly sensitive person, I have felt the impact of many auras in one space. One of the places I experience it is the airport. People are rushing around and often feeling stress. It's a place devoted to movement, and that's a lot of chaotic energy at times.

I've also experienced enjoyable moments in crowds as well. For example, I saw Taylor Swift in concert while I was writing this book. The people who were there were mostly excited and happy to be there. The show was spectacular, and it delighted the fans, so the energy of many thousands of people in the space had a celebratory feeling.

In that type of situation, there is a composite field generated by the crowd, the performers, and the crew. Everyone is working together to achieve or experience something. The auras of each person involved joins together to create a collaborative aura of interconnection via the shared experience and proximity.

Some songs had an emotional quality and a lot of sentimental significance to some of the attendees. Perhaps the songs embodied feelings that they had about break-ups or life changes that were able to facilitate their expression of those emotions. In those cases, the collective aura had some pretty strong frequencies of that healing. Even on social media, you would see them posting themselves crying and having a cathartic experience during the concert. The artist was sharing her creative expression likely derived from having a similar experience and was able to help other people access and release those feelings.

Being in group settings and being aware of your aura and energy as well as that of other people allows you to develop discernment. Discernment helps you distinguish what feels good to you and what does not. During those more emotional songs at the concert, I chose to seal my auric space and not absorb the emotions of other people. As an empath, that's very important for me. There are people who could be in a situation like that and feel impervious to it. For some, it might've resonated at that time and it could help them move energy that might've been stuck.

With emotional states, it's all about understanding your preferences and what you like to feel. Some people like to roll around in the mud, and that can feel cathartic and help them move energy-related to traumas in the past.

A big part of our experience of group settings from an auric perspective is our degree of sensitivity. Dr. Elaine Aron wrote a beautiful set of books about the highly sensitive person. Sensitivity levels are varied. It's also a continuum of moment-to-moment states and levels of sensitivity. We tend to feel even more sensitive or overstimulated when we're tired, hungry, dehydrated, or experiencing a lot of mental or emotional stress.

That would be a time to be extra conscientious about sealing your auric space in a crowded area so you can maintain your frequency and not be impacted by the frequency of others. Sometimes the impacts of other frequencies can be positive if they're raising yours. That's why it usually comes down to discernment.

PROTECTING
YOUR AURA

Creating protection for your aura in a crowd is an incredibly useful skill. You can use it to help maintain high-vibrational energy in your being. This translates into maintaining good health, wealth, and happiness. As we begin to understand the way that our electromagnetic field is affected by the electromagnetic fields of others, we can notice when we want to keep our frequency strong. Sometimes, we need to do that in situations where we experience fear or anxiety. When we feel worried about driving our car at a fast speed or other things that could be provoking, we need to assess first if there's anything that we need to do for safety.

Once we're confident we've addressed all safety precautions in a way that is practical and thorough, then we can notice if we are feeling any fear. We want to replace any feelings of fear with a feeling of freedom.

You are a being with free will. You have the ability to make choices for your highest good. If you have made all the choices that ensure your safety from a practical standpoint, then there is no use for fear. Fear can be helpful when we need to take action to maintain our security. Beyond that, it's low-vibrational energy. From a traditional Chinese medicine standpoint, it tends to cause stagnation or provocation in the kidney and bladder channels.

Even in the face of something that scares us or something that's challenging, we can infuse our electromagnetic field with good feelings and thoughts and use that as a tool to keep our frequency high.

It can be a good idea to protect your aura, which also ends up protecting your body. It's a way of fully inhabiting your electromagnetic field and taking ownership of the fact that you get to set the boundaries and choose the experience and energies that enter your auric egg. In the process below, you will learn how to do just that.

SEALING YOUR SPACE

When you seal up your personal space, the intention is that all that is for your highest good can enter the permeable membrane surrounding your aura. All that is not for your highest good will not enter and simply bounce off. This will take no additional effort from you beyond the invocation that I'll teach you below. I recommend memorizing this because then you can use it anytime, like when you walk into an airport or a grocery store. At first, you might keep it on a notecard in your wallet or in the Notes app on your phone. That way, you can easily access it and invoke it whenever you need it.

To enact the process, simply repeat the words in quotes below. You can say them out loud if you're in a situation where that is possible. Or you can say them in your mind, and they'll be equally as effective.

I learned a version of this process from my late medicine teacher, Laurie. I've adapted it over the years, and you can feel free to do the same. You'll get the idea, and you can change any words that feel good to you. We tried to create a comprehensive paragraph that would deal with anything and everything in all dimensions and make sure that our spaces are pristine.

When you state the words below, you can envision a swirl of high-vibrational energy starting just above the top of your aura and swirling down around it in a spiral until it reaches just below the bottom of your aura. You can also start from the bottom and move to the top. It might be different at times.

Say this: "I seal and protect all wormholes, portals, doorways, and openings in my aura and physical and energetic bodies in all dimensions and interdimensions and all realities as needed for my highest good and the highest good of all life, for all time. I own my space and only that which is of the light may enter. It is done."

You can use this is often as you like. I sometimes recommend it to parents of children who are old enough to understand, and they say this before bed to help with frightening dreams. It's nice for everyone, and it often creates an even better sleep experience.

OWN YOUR PERSONAL SPACE AND POWER TO MANIFEST SUCCESS

We've been exploring many facets of our auras and understanding how these fields around us influence our entire lives. We've also been exploring how our fields interact with other their fields when we are in proximity to other people. Sometimes, that can be a wonderful experience. And sometimes we can feel overwhelmed. If someone is a highly sensitive person or has an empathetic nature, it can be a challenge to be around other people. But even if that's not the case, having good boundaries from an energetic and auric perspective is critical not only to our health and well-being but also to our ability to thrive and be successful.

When we fully embody our own essence, which extends out through the entirety of our electromagnetic field, we can be filled with fortitude. In that embodiment, we own our space. When we own our space and fill it with our individual essence, then we are less able to be influenced by outside forces. If our intention is to remain open to expansive high-frequency energies, we're able to bring those into our being, even if we are filling our own space.

When our consciousness is seated in our being and electromagnetic field, we are able to alter it to our desires at any time. Owning our space does not in any way limit our growth potential. It doesn't limit or minimize our ability to integrate more higher-frequency energies into our fields. It helps us embody our intentional energy to attract more of it so higher-frequency energies integrate into our being. Owning our space and filling our energy field and auras with our own unique individual essence allows us to be unscathed by the experiences of life.

It is not only an energetic reality; it's a mindset and a way of living. Here's an example: think about when you're out driving and experience a driver who has mild road rage, so they are honking and beeping or tailgating you, wanting you to go faster. Some people get bothered by this. It affects them, and then through that reaction, they've essentially lowered their frequency. They let the frequency of anger that the other driver is carrying impact their being. The other driver is in a car, but don't think for any moment that their auric field and its density is not interacting with yours, sort of pushing on it in that situation.

However, another scenario is that same thing occurs, and you just chuckle and move on with your day, driving safely and relaxed. The aura filled with anger may brush up against yours in that interaction, but it didn't affect you. If you own your space and are filling your space with your own energy, then your edges are stronger. Your boundaries are more solid.

This is energetic, and it's also translated into the way we behave and experience life. So, the same person with those strong energetic boundaries because they filled their space with their individual essence is also able to interact with other people in a way that doesn't throw them off their center.

We are going to fortify that side of you in this chapter and then explore and utilize the fact that when your energy field is permeated by your individual high-frequency essence, you have the ability to better manifest success in your life. You can manifest anything you desire. And high-frequency essences can carry the vibration of victory. You can own a victorious energy and seed it in your space. Then, as you walk through life each day, you are emitting the frequency of victory. Success contains that energy, and it's not about competition. It's about the win-win essence of high-frequency living. It is being in a place that your auric field so strongly emits success and it is so fortified with strength that you are then in an effortless space of manifesting success.

Our first step will be getting you aligned with owning your space at all times. Then, we will be harnessing that power to create success in your career and life.

OWN YOUR SPACE TO CREATE SUCCESS MEDITATION

Take some deep breaths and get in a centered and relaxed space. The reason we often begin our activities and meditations in this book with breathing is to bring us back into presence in the physical body. In this case, we will extend that to greater levels of being present.

Feel present in your body and bring your awareness to the edges of your body so you have a feeling of fullness of your being and everything contained within your body. Next, bring that awareness out your edges. See if you can feel all your edges simultaneously, so that means bring your awareness into the bottom of your feet and the top of your head and the palms of your hands all at the same time. Take some time and get to the point where you bring your awareness to the entire outside edge of your body. Can you feel all the surface area simultaneously? At first, you can cycle your awareness through different areas of your body until you're able to feel them all at once. Notice your hands, then your back, then your calves, then the top of your head. Make the areas larger as you cycle through so eventually you can sense them all simultaneously. This may take a little time. No need to rush.

Next, begin to notice your auric egg. It's the oval-shaped bubble of your electromagnetic field that extends out around you three feet in all directions. Feel that space and bring your attention from the outside edges of your physical body to the edges of that electromagnetic field. Feel those edges and practice the same cycling through areas as needed. Take some time and get to the point where you can feel all those edges of that auric egg around you completely. Feel it in totality. You might need to cycle your awareness between front and back, left and right, bottom and top until you can feel all of it.

Next, we are going to bring you into ownership of your space. This whole bubble and everything inside it is 100 percent yours. It's nobody else's. You own it. It's your space. It's meant to be infused with your essence.

Sometimes throughout our lives, including childhood, this space gets impacted. It can be a time when our boundaries were not respected or another energetic impingement on our field. In a perfect situation, the bubble would repel all that, and if not, it would bounce right back out. A lot of times we have areas in our auras that we are not fully embodying in our entirety. To shift that, we move into ownership of our space intentionally because it's the first step to taking control of our lives and existences on a deep level. That means taking full responsibility for our entire energy field.

When we take 100 percent responsibility for ourselves, our lives, and our energy, we can create it exactly as we choose. It's a beautiful, exciting responsibility. It means that we can create and experience whatever we desire. It has a lot of translations in our day-to-day life, but today we will work on it from the standpoint of our energy body and our success.

Feel the totality of your auric egg. You are going to use a powerful affirmative statement and infuse your auric egg and your being with it until you feel it on your most primal and profound level. State aloud, "I own my space." Repeat that phrase to yourself quietly over and over. Maybe you need to yell it or say it loudly. You can make gestures with your arms and legs out to the edges of your aura as you say it to punctuate the intention as needed. Keep repeating it over and over so you feel it. Repeat it as you bring your attention to the edges of your auric egg again. Hold that focus of that edge of your field, repeating the statement and infusing the entirety of the space with it. You own your space. Keep repeating this and working with it until it feels solid. I recommend you do this daily for a quick minute or so or whenever you think of it as needed.

Next, were going to bring your powerful intention to bear. Your next statement, which you will announce with authority and intention aloud, is, "I own my life." State that: "I own my life. I own my space, and I own my life." Repeat those phrases to yourself and feel how ownership of your life encompasses the energy fields around your home(s), your car(s), and everything you do and everywhere you go. This ownership of your life does not impinge on anybody else. It simply is a strong and fortified energy that keeps you in energetic structural integrity. It helps you hold your boundaries and stand in your strength and power.

Take a moment to feel the difference in your auric egg, your physical body, and your entire energy body. Feel that difference of owning your space and owning your life. Use those statements frequently to affirm these intentions, and they will become habit and a constant reality for you.

Now, we're going to allow this strength, fortitude, and power in your energetic space to outwardly project success into every facet of your life. This will be especially pertinent for your career, and it should also help you open avenues to opportunities and wealth.

Repeat aloud: "I own my space, and I own my life." Bring your attention so you're once again feeling the edges of your auric egg and repeating the statement. Now, call forth the power of victory and success. You will do this with the help of two powerful spirit guides. You can invoke others, too, as you choose. Call forth the Greek goddess Nike, goddess of victory. And call forth Lakshmi, the goddess of good fortune from Vedic and Hindu mythology. State aloud, "Nike and Lakshmi, please come and visit me now. I request the honor of your presence."

Feel yourself there in your auric egg, owning your space. Notice Nike and Lakshmi before you and their energy fields and how they are owning their space. Feel how they are mirroring that back to you in the way that they each own their space. In this exercise, their auras will interact with your aura in a positive way. This can still occur even when you're owning your space because it allows in all that will enhance you and all that is for your highest good and simply screens out that which is not.

You can greet the goddesses in your own words and thank them for their help. Next, state aloud to them both, "I now invoke high-vibrational success and wealth into my being. I am living the frequency of victory and success, and my career is optimal and exactly what I desire deep in my heart. I am unlimited and easily create whatever I choose."

Next, state aloud to the goddesses, "Please make this so in every level of my being and in all realities for all time for my highest good and the highest good of all life."

Feel the statement and this energy echoing through your aura. Witness golden energy flowing from Nike. Watch hot pink and lots of bright, vibrant, jewel-toned energies flowing from Lakshmi. See these energies swirl together before you, around you, through your body, through your aura, and out into the world. Repeat the statement, "I own my space, and I embody success." Say it over and over as you feel these energies infuse you and surround you. You have invited these powerful success goddesses to infuse you with very high-vibrational energy. Feel gratitude and appreciation for the moment and let it seep into your being.

You can have a communication and discussion with the goddesses now, asking them for anything else you would like and thanking them. You can ask to exchange energy with them even more if you would like, and you can invite their auras to be in contact with your aura even more by placing your hands in your lap, palms up, and inviting each goddess in turn to hover her spirit hands over yours, feeling the pulsing and exchange of energy between you two. You can dialogue with the goddesses and communicate with them for as long as you'd like.

Eventually, thank them and state the following: "This activity now ceases. All that transpired was, is, and will always be for the highest good of all life. I am so grateful and thankful for the help and the raising of my frequency. I appreciate the bounty of my life."

This is a powerful exercise, and you can enact it as frequently as you desire. You can work with these goddesses and the idea of owning your space to magnify these frequencies in your life every day if you choose. You can also do this once, and set it and forget it. This energy now permanently remains in your being, and as long as you keep your frequency high, it will continue to do so. You can use the affirmative statement "I am success" to embody that frequency.

THE FAMILY AURA

From the time children are born and through their seventh year, on some level their aura and body is partially contained within the aura of their biological mother. This phenomenon occurs whether the mom and baby are together or apart. There are times, in the case of adoption, when the child's bond is strong to a new parental figure and that auric connection is transferred to that person. In my twenties, I worked as a kindergarten teacher for eight years, and I have a degree in education. At that time, I was also already working part-time as a medical intuitive and was actively training with my medicine teacher. My intuitive senses were open and increasing. I had a chance to observe the idea of a child having a certain level of auric containment and the safety and security that came from that on an energetic level. It served to help the child feel physically and emotionally safe.

There are certainly numerous cases where children unfortunately are not in secure homes with loving family for all kinds of reasons. This family aura usually exists in the more ideal situations. In addition to the very close intrinsic, auric bond with the mother, there is also an overall family aura contained around a family that lives in the same home together. It is amplified if it's either a biologically related family or a close family with feelings of deep emotional connection.

The desire to be inside the safety of the family aura combined with the primal fear of the dark is one of the big reasons children want to sleep in their parents' bedrooms at night. They want to be in the bubble of the family, which is a composite aura from everyone in the family, and they ask especially the parents. Little kids feel even safer in the personal space of their parents. Those of us who are fortunate enough to recall time spent with our parents when we were little in the feeling of emotional safety and total acceptance have experienced this on an intrinsic level.

Something to notice as we grow into adults is that in families where that auric bond and interconnection is especially strong, we may need to be vigilant about owning our personal space as adults and defining our existence outside of the family aura. We will learn how to do this over time while still enjoying and feeling grateful for the incredible gift of a loving family.

For those who did not grow up with a nurturing family or a sense of safety, the opportunity is to create that for oneself individually through meaningful connections. For everybody, it can also be helpful to feel your spirit family and the benevolent, loving spirit guides who are always available to be your family. For example, I have felt for the past 27 years like the archangels are part of my family. I adopt them and they adopt me. The archangels are every human's family because they're part of us. They have devoted a portion of their attention to the earth and humanity for the entirety of the existence of both. The archangels are all part of the human family. Connect with them today and feel their love. Get to know them and build your connection with them.

WHAT HAPPENS TO AURAS DURING SEX

Auras undergo all kinds of interesting movement during physical intimacy. The photons in the body get very active and move along paths in ways that are unique during that time. All kinds of feel-good chemicals are being released and sensations are being experienced, so the electromagnetic field of each person has a lot of distinctive qualities at that point. Plus, you're mixing the auras of two people together often infused with feelings of passion, romance, and love, so the auras reflect that and interact with each other. When people are physically interacting and experiencing sensations in the body, the auras are doing the same type of thing.

Take note during an encounter when it feels right and enlist your partner's participation. Notice what is happening with your auras as you move closer to one another and then engage in physical intimacy. Feel your energetic bubble around you and then feel how your partner is inside it and you are inside theirs. The closeness creates auric intimacy as well as bodily intimacy. When there is emotional connection and romantic love, you can feel those frequencies in each of your auras and how they feed into one another. Take time to observe your auras during physical intimacy and share that experience with your partner. You may find that it helps you understand each other even more deeply.

AURA PLAY WITH A ROMANTIC PARTNER

If you and your intimate partner would like to engage in some conscious auric energy play, you can try the following activity. Make sure you're both centered and do some deep breathing. Take time connecting and gazing into each other's eyes and stating each of your intentions for the experience. Make sure you express love and appreciation for each other to set a high-vibrational tone to the encounter. You might also decide to have the intention that the encounter will be joyful and playful. Perhaps the flavor you both would like to experience would be one of emotional connection or intense passion. You can try different intentions with this.

Face one another and notice the way that your auras are interacting before you begin physical touch. Share your perceptions. Move into the experience, pausing periodically and sharing what you notice and feel in your aura and the joint aura of your experience.

You can also do some of the physical maneuvers you would do during physical intimacy, except without actually touching, and allow the energy to move between you through your auras. See if you can sense it. Take turns playing with that energy. Make it like a game. The object is to have your partner feel your touch without you physically touching them. Sense your auras. Consider it an exploration together.

As you progress through the acts of physical intimacy, keep noticing what happens to your auras. And when you're in intense physical union, set the intention to observe what happens to your auras during that time too. For that brief time, do your two auras become one? If so, to what degree? Is it total or partial? What does it feel like when that occurs?

If you or your partner experience orgasm, try to notice what happens to the aura at that time. You can also notice these types of auric conditions and changes if you are practicing solo intimacy. And it would apply in intimate situations involving more than two people as well.

After the experience is complete, talk to each other about what you both experienced and share your thoughts and feelings. Use this activity as an opportunity to create even deeper intimacy.

THE TAOIST THREE TREASURES

In Taoist tradition, there is a branch of study devoted to sacred sex and intimacy. Sometimes, you will hear it referred to as *solo* and *dual cultivation*. It is about management of energy in the body and circulating it intentionally. The intention is often for healing. Although the Taoists didn't speak about in great detail about the aura, it was acknowledged. When we think about the concept that we have of the aura, which is the result of the movement of photons through the body, we can see how conscious circulation of energy in the body could and often does have a significant effect on the aura.

One of the many Taoist practices refers to three significant areas of the body called the three treasures. The three treasures are energy centers in the body especially associated with cultivating consciousness and intimacy.

The first treasure is often referred to as the Jing. It exists in the lower abdomen, down to the base of the spine. It's your power center and a seed of sensual activity. It's a radiating, pulsing center that encompasses the physical body in that area.

The next one is referred to as the Qi. This is the center of the chest area. A lot of us would think of it is associated with the heart or love.

The third is often referred to as the Shen. It's located in the brow center and back into the brain.

You can think of these centers existing centered along the midline of the body, not only left to right but also front to back. So, their cores are right along where the spine would be, and they radiate out significantly through most if not all the body in that area. You can picture them as sphere shapes. These are all associated with numerous meridians and energy channels in Taoist philosophy.

Taoists and people who are learning solo or dual cultivation often practice meditation and focus circulating their energy between these three areas. Then they learn how to harness those during sexual activity to experience transcendence. With a partner, there is an option to use the centers to connect even more deeply and enhance the sacred communion of sexual intimacy. There is a lot of effect on the aura when we do this!

Below I'll share some brief instructions on something I refer to as the triple infinity technique. This is something you could try with a partner.

You can also meditate and focus on these energy centers solo and notice what solo intimacy does with these centers. Then bring your attention to where the centers radiate out into your aura and what happens when you move the energy between the centers and how it affects the aura. When you engage in solo intimacy, the movement of photons changes in the body. How does it affect the aura? If you perceive visually, then you may see lots of interesting things happen in your aura during that time.

THE TRIPLE INFINITY TECHNIQUE

Have your partner sit cross-legged up against a wall or headboard with several large pillows behind their back. This can be on the bed or a clean carpeted floor. Have them reach behind their back and raise the pillow up off the floor while you slip into their lap and wrap your legs around their back. Your feet will go where the pillow was. They can then let the pillows go and lean back.

You should be sitting so the front of your bodies are flush together from base to chest. You can place a pillow under your backside as needed for comfort. Embrace and relax.

As you hug each other, let your minds become quiet, like you are meditating together. Notice each other's breathing. In time, bring your attention three key areas of the body:

1. The abdomen area—Jing

2. The center of the chest or heart center—Qi

3. The "third eye" area between the eyes encompassing the center of the forehead—Shen

Feel each area in turn. Notice the connection between you in each area. It may feel like pulsing or tingling. Let there be a gentle feeling of an infinity symbol in each of the three areas circling between your bodies, hearts, and minds.

Notice how this feels in your aura and your partner's aura. You've put your two bodies in very close proximity, so you're occupying a lot of the same auric space. When you add the triple infinity technique, what happens to your auras? What do you sense emotionally? What thoughts occur to you? What's happening in the outer parts of your auras? When you put your forehead near one another, are you picking up on the flavor and thoughts that the movement of photons in your partner's brain are emitting? Do you feel it as it emanates out from their cranium, into their aura, and into yours? Do you feel that translate through your brain?

When you tune in to the center of the chest and the tiny amount of space between you there, even if it's only where your shoulders are concave, there is empty space that's full of your auras. Is it a shared aura at this time? Do you feel a certain flavor to the energy shared in the aura around both of your bodies? Does it have an emotional or love-based flavor? Or something else? Are there colors, sounds, music, or anything in particular that you notice in the space around your bodies and between your bodies especially in that area?

Bring your attention the base of your spine and low abdomen area. There are little pockets of empty space between you there. Sense into that part of your aura. Does it feel like shared auric space? Feel the area around your bodies in that lower-body zone. Because you're sitting, your legs and feet will sort of be entwined. Notice physical body and empty space in that area. Do you feel a certain creative power from yourself or your partner? What happens when those energies share the same physical location? Notice how it feels and observe the space around your hips. Feel your aura and your partners. Notice any sensations.

Take as long as you'd like to experience this delightful activity together, and when you are ready and have concluded your session of intimate activity, make sure you take some time to share your experiences with each other to further build your intimate bond.

WISHING YOU JOY ON YOUR AURA JOURNEY

I am so pleased you took this journey with me! You have learned all the skills you will need to completely overhaul your aura and create the life you desire. Keep practicing the techniques that we learned, and you will become even more proficient. The management of personal power and energy is a skill, and you can become masterful at it. I'm so excited that you have gathered all this wonderful knowledge and experience. I can't wait to hear how it's enhanced your life. Find me on Instagram @AmyLeighMercree or chat with me through my website, AmyLeighMercree.com. I'd love to hear your experiences with the activities in this book, and I can't wait to learn what you've discovered.

You can also get the special tool kit I created for you to go with this book by going to amyleighmercree.com /auraalchemyresources. May your aura be alchemized and your life unfold with joy and success. Sending you love and hugs!

BIBLIOGRAPHY

Aron, Elaine. *The Highly Sensitive Person: How to Thrive When the World Overwhelms You.* New York: Harmony Books, 1997.

Beaty, William. "Electricity Is *Not* a Form of Energy." Accessed May 12, 2023. http://amasci.com/miscon/energ1.html.

Brook, Pete. "Aura Portraits Make Good Art, Bad Science." *Wired*, February 25, 2011.

Cayce, Edward. *Auras: An Essay on the Meaning of Colors.* Virginia Beach, VA: A.R.E. Press, 1973.

Conniff, Richard. "Alchemy May Not Have Been the Pseudoscience We All Thought It Was." *Smithsonian*, 2014. https://www.smithsonianmag .com/history/alchemy-may-not-been-pseudoscience-we-thought-it -was-180949430/.

Crease, Robert P. "The Bizarre Logic of the Many-Worlds Theory." *Nature*, September 2, 2019.

Domain of Science. "The Map of Particle Physics: The Stanford Model Explained." YouTube video, 31:47, May 1, 2021. https://www.youtube .com/watch?v=mYcLuWHzfmE

EM and RF Testing Solutions. "EMF & RF Testing." Accessed May 18, 2021. http://www.emfrf.com/.

"How the Human Body Creates Electromagnetic Fields." Forbes. November 3, 2017. a. https://www.forbes.com/sites/quora/2017/11/03/ how-the-human-body-creates-electromagnetic-fields/?sh=482df8e056ea

Gupta, Shiwangi, R. S. Sharma, and R. Singh. "Non-Ionizing Radiation as Possible Carcinogen." *International Journal of Environmental Health Research* 32 (2020): 1–25.

Hammerschlag, Richard, et al. "Biofield Physiology: A Framework for an Emerging Discipline." *Global Advances in Health and Medicine* 4 (2015): 35–41.

Havas, Magda. "When Theory and Observation Collide: Can Non-Ionizing Radiation Cause Cancer?" *Environmental Pollution* 221 (2017): 501–5.

Helmenstine, Anne Marie. "The Relationship between Electricity and Magnetism." *Thought Co.*, December 2, 2022.

Hess, Katie. *Flowerevolution: Blooming into Your Full Potential with the Magic of Flowers*. Carlsbad, CA: Hay House, 2016.

Laozi. *The Way of Lao Tzu*. Translated by Wing-Tsit Chan. Pearson, 1963.

Looking Glass Universe. "I Did the Double Slit Experiment at Home." YouTube video, 15:25, November 11, 2022. https://www.youtube.com /watch?v=v_uBaBuarEM&ab_channel=LookingGlassUniverse.

Mercola, Joseph. *EMF*d: 5G, Wi-Fi & Cell Phones: Hidden Harms and How to Protect Yourself*. Carlsbad, CA: Hay House, 2021.

Mercree, Amy Leigh. *A Little Bit of Goddess: An Introduction to the Divine Feminine*. New York: Sterling Ethos, 2019.

———*A Little Bit of Meditation: An Introduction to Mindfulness*. New York: Sterling Ethos, 2017.

———*Essential Oils Handbook: Recipes for Natural Living*. New York: Sterling Ethos, 2018.

———*The Healing Home: A Room-by-Room Guide to Positive Vibes*. New York: Sterling Ethos, 2022.

———*The Spiritual Girl's Guide to Dating: Your Enlightened Path to Love, Sex, and Soul Mates*. Avon, MA: Adams Media, 2012.

Mercree, Amy Leigh and Chad Mercree. *A Little Bit of Chakras: An Introduction to Energy Healing*. New York: Sterling Ethos, 2016.

Milán et al. "Auras in Mysticism and Synaesthesia: A Comparison." *Consciousness and Cognition* 21 (2012): 258–68.

Mildon, Emma. *Evolution of Goddess: A Modern Girl's Guide to Activating Your Feminine Superpowers*. New York: Enliven Books, 2018.

Miller et al. "Risks to Health and Well-Being from Radio-Frequency Radiation Emitted by Cell Phones and Other Wireless Devices." *Frontiers in Public Health* 7 (2019): 223.

Mortazavi et al. "The Fundamental Reasons Why Laptop Computers Should Not Be Used on Your Lap." *Journal of Biomedical Physics & Engineering* 6 (2016): 279–84.

Murphy-Hiscock, Arin. *The Green Witch: Your Complete Guide to the Natural Magic of Herbs, Flowers, Essential Oils, and More*. New York: Adams Media, 2017.

NASA Science. "Anatomy of an Electromagnetic Wave." Last updated June 1, 2023. https://science.nasa.gov/ems/02_anatomy.

National Cancer Institute. "Electromagnetic Fields & Cancer." May 12, 2023. https://www.cancer.gov/about-cancer/causes-prevention/risk /radiation/electromagnetic-fields-fact-sheet.

National Institute of Environmental Health Sciences. "Electric & Magnetic Fields." Accessed May 18, 2021. https://www.niehs.nih.gov/ health/topics/agents/emf/index.cfm.

O'Neill, Claire. "A Camera That Sees Your True Colors?" NPR: The Picture Show. June 23, 2012. https://www.npr.org/sections/pictureshow /2012/07/23/157095250/a-camera-that-sees-your-true-colors.

PBS. "Basics of Buddhism." https://www.pbs.org/edens/thailand /buddhism.htm.

Pehek, John O., Harry J. Kyler, and David L. Faust. "Image Modulation in Corona Discharge Photography: Moisture Is a Principal Determinant of the Form and Color of Kirlian Photographs of Human Subjects." *Science* 194 (1976): 263–70.

Pineault, Nicolas. *The Non-Tinfoil Guide to EMFs: How to Fix Our Stupid Use of Technology*. CreateSpace Independent Publishing Platform, 2017.

Pitchford, Paul. *Healing with Whole Foods: Asian Traditions and Modern Nutrition*. Berkeley, California: North Atlantic Books. 2002.

Reichstein, Gail. *Wood Becomes Water: Chinese Medicine in Everyday Life*. New York: Kodansha America. 1998.

Roberts, Andrew P. "Magnetic Mineral Diagenesis." *Earth-Science Reviews* 151 (2015): 1–47. https://www.sciencedirect.com/science/article/abs/pii/ S0012825215300453.

Rosenblum, Sam and Isabelle K. Brownfield. "Magnetic Susceptibilities of Minerals." U.S. Geological Survey Open-File Report 99-0529. https://pubs.usgs.gov/of/1999/ofr-99-0529/.

Rubik et al. "Biofield Science and Healing: History, Terminology, and Concepts." *Global Advances in Health and Medicine* 4 (2015): 8–14.

Rudolf Steiner Archive. "Theosophy: Chapter III: The Three Worlds: 6: Thought Forms and the Human Aura." May 12, 2023. https://rsarchive .org/Books/GA009/English/AP1971/GA009_c03_6.html.

ScienceDaily. "Electrical Activity in Living Organisms Mirrors Electrical Fields in Atmosphere." May 5, 2020. https://www.sciencedaily.com /releases/2020/05/200505121642.htm.

Stanley, Tracee. *Radiant Rest: Yoga Nidra for Deep Relaxation & Awakened Clarity*. Boulder, Colorado: Shambhala, 2021.

Theosophy World Resource Center. "Aura." May 11, 2023. https://www .theosophy.world/encyclopedia/aura.

Van Wijk, Roeland and Eduard P. A. Van Wijk. "An Introduction to Human Biophoton Emission." *Forsch Komplementarmed Klass Naturheilkd* 2 (2005): 77–83.

Wolchover, Natalie, S. Velasco, and L. Reading. "A New Map of All the Particles and Forces." *Quanta Magazine*. October 22, 2020. https://www .quantamagazine.org/a-new- map-of-the-standard-model-of-particle -physics-20201022/.

ACKNOWLEDGMENTS

I have been incredibly fortunate to have so many helpful people in my life. There were teachers sprinkled through my school experience who understood different types of learning and ignited my imagination and love for science, mythology, writing, and much more. Those teachers like Mr. Buteau and Mrs. Broussard seeded some of the ideas that blossomed into this book. In Mr. Buteau's sixth-grade science class, my fascination with what we now call quantum mechanics officially began. It offered me some understanding that started to offer me context for what I was already perceiving on a visionary level.

In seventh grade, Mrs. Broussard opened the worlds of mythology and ancient history to me in a way that was exciting and captured my imagination then and still has many decades later. I'm so grateful to those teachers who took the time and showed kindness and understanding and shared their enthusiasm.

When I was 18, I was lucky enough to meet my late medicine teacher, Laurie, and embark upon a process of deep healing and eventually become her apprentice. She gave me the foundation that has enabled me to do my job on a spiritual and shamanic level.

In 2008, life really smiled on me and put my fabulous literary agent, Lisa Hagan, into my path. I'm so thankful for Lisa on so many levels. She's believed in me and tirelessly championed my career. She's become a dear friend.

And she's always seen the possibilities in my dharmic work and supported helping me share it with the world.

Speaking of seeing potential, Allison Janice, acquiring editor for Hay House, is an angel incarnate in my life! She saw the potential of my work and visionary particle physics content and worked to get the Hay House team to see it too.

The blessings continued when I got to work with my wonderful editor, Ashten Evans! I was fortunate to work with Ashten in the past on other projects, and what a delightful surprise that seems very synchronistic to get to work with her again.

Many thanks to everyone at Hay House who made this book possible! I'd like to thank the talented designers that made this book so beautiful, Sending much gratitude to the sales and marketing teams for getting the book noticed and into so many hands! I'd like to share my gratitude with the whole team at Hay House. Thank you to the executive team and the editorial team for supporting this project. I'm so grateful for your help and direction.

I'm truly grateful for the support of my numerous wonderful colleagues over the years. Kate Zimmerman has been a guiding light in my career as an author, and I am forever grateful to her. All my author friends who have been there sharing ideas, supporting one another: what a gift you are. Life is so much more fun when we have friends surrounding us on the journey! Thank you for being there.

I am beyond thankful for my close friends and family. You've all provided the emotional support, nurturing, and community that has made me who I am today. My brother and sister-in-law and loving extended family are such a gift. My parents have been my most steadfast supporters, and I am truly fortunate to be so blessed to have them in my life. Thank you all.

ABOUT THE
AUTHOR

Amy Leigh Mercree is an internationally acclaimed medical intuitive with over 20 years of experience. She specializes in spirit guides with a focus on shamanism, healing your home, and holistic wellness. Using a combination of spirituality and science, Amy's job is finding the root of imbalances in the body. Clients come to her with health issues that they have not had results healing elsewhere, and Amy helps them to get to the absolute root of the problem and put together a plan for how to fix it. She's helped thousands of people find the causes of numerous mild and moderate medical conditions and uncover their body's wisdom to heal permanently.

Amy is a best-selling author of 17 books, journals, and card decks. She is a media personality, holistic health expert, and mystic teacher. She instructs internationally sharing Meet Your Goddess Guides, Ancestral and Karmic Shamanism, and Medical Intuitive Apprenticeship Certification.

Mercree has been featured in *Glamour*, *Women's Health*, *Shape*, *HuffPost*, YourTango, *Soul & Spirit*, MindBodyGreen, CBS, NBC, Hello Giggles, *Reader's Digest*, *The Oprah Magazine*, *Forbes*, ABC, *First for Women*, *Country Living*, CW, Fox, *Bustle*, Well+Good, Refinery 29, Hello Glow,

SheKnows, Thrive Global, Spartan, Poosh, *Parade*, Oprah-Daily, and many more.

Mercree is the author of *The Spiritual Girl's Guide to Dating; A Little Bit of Chakras: An Introduction to Energy Healing; Joyful Living: 101 Ways to Transform Your Spirit and Revitalize Your Life; The Compassion Revolution: 30 Days of Living from the Heart; The Chakras and Crystals Cookbook: Juices, Smoothies, Sorbets, Salads, and Crystal Infusions to Empower Your Energy Centers; A Little Bit of Meditation: An Introduction to Mindfulness; Recipes for Natural Living: Essential Oils Handbook; Recipes for Natural Living: Apple Cider Vinegar Handbook; A Little Bit of Mindfulness: An Introduction to Being Present; The Mood Book: Crystals, Oils, and Rituals to Elevate Your Spirit; A Little Bit of Goddess: An Introduction to the Divine Feminine; A Little Bit of Chakras: Your Personal Path to Energy Healing; A Little Bit of Meditation: Your Personal Path to Mindfulness; A Little Bit of Mindfulness: Your Personal Path to Awareness; 100 Days to Calm: A Journal for Finding Everyday Tranquility; The Healing Home: A Room-by-Room Guide to Positive Vibes;* and *Blissful Baths: 40 Rituals for Self-Care and Relaxation.*

Connect with Amy at AmyLeighMercree.com and @AmyLeighMercree on Instagram, TikTok, Facebook, and Pinterest. Get Amy's special tool kit to support you in your auric learning quest. It has audio meditations from the book, playlists of music to cue up when you are clearing your aura, and playlists for when we manifest our dream lives together using auric particles. Plus, it has color charts to reference when you are perceiving auras, audio mediations for each chakra to connect with their auric energies, and lots of other fun bonuses just for you! Get it at **amyleighmercree.com/auraalchemyresources**.

SUGGESTED FURTHER READING

Angel Tech: A Modern Shaman's Guide to Reality Selection by Antero Alli and Dr. Robert Anton Wilson

The Non-Tinfoil Guide to EMFs: How to Fix Our Stupid Use of Technology by Nicolas Pineault

Creating Affluence: The A-to-Z Steps to a Richer Life by Deepak Chopra

A Little Bit of Goddess: An Introduction to the Divine Feminine by Amy Leigh Mercree

The Healing Home: A Room-by-Room Guide to Positive Vibes by Amy Leigh Mercree

The Highly Sensitive Person by Dr. Elaine Aron

Healing with Whole Foods: Asian Traditions and Modern Nutrition by Paul Pitchford

Money, and the Law of Attraction: Learning to Attract Wealth, Health, and Happiness by Esther and Jerry Hicks

The Dental Diet by Dr. Steven Lin

A Little Bit of Chakras: An Introduction to Energy Healing by Chad and Amy Leigh Mercree

The Big Leap by Gay Hendricks

Wood Becomes Water: Chinese Medicine in Everyday Life by Gail Reichstein, Robert Rex, Jessica DePete MS Lac

Acupuncture Points Handbook: A Patient's Guide to the Locations and Functions of over 400 Acupuncture Points by Deborah Bleecker

The Moon Under Her Feet by Clysta Kinstler

We hope you enjoyed this Hay House book. If you'd like to receive
our online catalog featuring additional information on Hay House
books and products, or if you'd like to find out more about the
Hay Foundation, please contact:

Hay House, Inc., P.O. Box 5100, Carlsbad, CA 92018-5100
(760) 431-7695 or (800) 654-5126
(760) 431-6948 (fax) or (800) 650-5115 (fax)
www.hayhouse.com® • www.hayfoundation.org

———

Published in Australia by: Hay House Australia Pty. Ltd.,
18/36 Ralph St., Alexandria NSW 2015
Phone: 612-9669-4299 • *Fax:* 612-9669-4144
www.hayhouse.com.au

Published in the United Kingdom by: Hay House UK, Ltd.,
The Sixth Floor, Watson House, 54 Baker Street, London W1U 7BU
Phone: +44 (0)20 3927 7290 • *Fax:* +44 (0)20 3927 7291
www.hayhouse.co.uk

Published in India by: Hay House Publishers India,
Muskaan Complex, Plot No. 3, B-2, Vasant Kunj, New Delhi 110 070
Phone: 91-11-4176-1620 • *Fax:* 91-11-4176-1630
www.hayhouse.co.in

———

Access New Knowledge.
Anytime. Anywhere.

Learn and evolve at your own pace
with the world's leading experts.

www.hayhouseU.com